ISBN 978-1-334-93631-9
PIBN 10781556

FB &c Ltd, Dalton House, 60 Windsor Avenue, London, SW19 2RR.
Company number 08720141. Registered in England and Wales.

For support please visit www.forgottenbooks.com

LOVE

AND

MADNESS;

A STORY TOO TRUE.

IN

SERIES OF LETTERS,

BETWEEN

Parties whoſe Names would perhaps be mentioned were they leſs known or leſs lamented.

GOVERNOR. "*Who did the bloody Deed?*
OROONOKO. "*The Deed was mine.*
"*Bloody I know it is; and I expect*
"*Your laws ſhould tell me ſo. Thus ſelf condemn'd,*
"*I do reſign myſelf into their hands;*
"*The hands of Juſtice.*"

OR. 5. 3.

HARTWELL. "*If this be not Love, it is Madneſs;*
and then, it is pardonable."

OLD, BAT.

DUBLIN:

PRINTED BY JAMES AND RICHARD BYRN, No. 18,
SYCAMORE-ALLEY,
FOR THE PROPRIETOR.

M.DCC.LXXX.

It is not neceſſary to ſay any thing by wa of *Preface*, than to deſire the Reader, wh feels an Inclination to cenſure any of theſ Letters, will recollect the Perſons by and t whom, and the Situations in which, the were written.

CONTENTS.

hint

32. Mr. H.

51. The

60. The

MEMOIRS OF MISS RAY.

(Not in the London Edition.)

The following Account of Miss Ray, *(said to be written by a Gentleman of this City*,) first appeared in the* Hibernian Magazine, *for* April, 1779, *and is now, by particular Desire, republished.*

Dublin, 20 Aug. 1780.

Illa, quis & me, inquit, miseram, & te perdidit, Orpheu?
Jamque vale: feror ingenti circumdata nocte,
Invalidasque tibi tendens, heu! non tua, palmas. Virg.

Then thus the *fair*: what fury seiz'd on thee,
Unhappy man! to lose thyself and me?
And now farewell! involv'd in shades of night,
For ever I am ravish'd from thy sight:
In vain I reach my feeble hands to join
In sweet embraces, ah! no longer thine! Dryden.

DID we live in the days of knight errantry, when the passion of love inspired its votaries with sentiments which frequently produced the most extraordinary effects, the transactions of which we are now to treat, might pass unnoticed; but the present polished and enlightened age has exploded as chimerical, ideas which are now to be found but in the rude

* Mr. Christopher Jackson.

legends

legends of the middle ages ;—serve to embellish the agreeable fictions of the poets ;—or to work up the wonderful and pathetic of a modern novel.

Illicit love now reigns triumphant, pervading all degrees, from the peer, (we had almost said prince,) to the peasant: obedient to its impulse, or the stronger dictates of interest, the fair ones of the present age submit their mercenary charms; and the men equally distinguished for dissipation and inconstancy, relinquish the happiness of a virtuous union, to violate the marriage bed ;—engage in the laudable pursuits of seduction ;—or revel in the arms of incontinent beauty.

The recent and deplorable act of Mr. Hackman, in whatever point of view it is considered, affords to those who make human nature the object of their study and enquiry, a remarkable incident in its history, — and a query naturally arises, which we shall, however, submit to the casuist ; — "Whether love and malice to the same object can dwell together in the same breast?" Mr. Hackman shot at Miss Ray because he loved her ; but how are we to reconcile the sentiment with the act? certain it is, that Miss Ray in the premature, and deplorable death, which she received by the hands of her admirer, experienced no less than she could expect or feel from the effects of his most deadly hate *.

That

* After the murder of Miss Ray, two letters were found in *Mr. Hackman's* pocket, one, a copy of a letter which he had written

That "enjoyment is the grave of desire,"—is an aphorism in love, better verified by experience than many in Hippocrates or Boerhaave; but, in direct contradiction to a generally received, and well-founded maxim, we find Mr. Hackman, after a long and particular intimacy with Miss Ray, during which she not only encouraged his addresses, but favoured him with that last proof of her esteem, by which those who are best acquainted with the female heart, must acknowledge, that the sincerity of women in matters of love, can only be truly ascertained; as it is also the most trying test of that constancy, which the men are apt to profess, but whose ultimate object is generally possession; and whose attentions and admiration is too frequently found to decrease from the time that object is attained. But Mr. Hackman's affection is said to have continued unchanged, and his attachment unalterably fixed, from the commencement of their amour, to its final, and fatal termination*.

Notwith-

written to Miss Ray, and the other to his brother-in-law, in Bow-street. The first of these epistles is replete with warm expressions of affection to the unfortunate object of his love, and an earnest recommendation of his passion. The other contains a pathetic relation of the melancholy resolution he had taken, and a confession of the cause that produced it.

* In the reign of the Emperor NERO, OCTAVIUS SAGITTA, tribune of the people, intoxicated with a passion for PONTIA POSTHUMIA, whom he had long enjoyed in the most unbounded degree of illicit intercourse, found his love so increased *by possession*, that he solicited her, with incessant importunity,

Notwithstanding the elevated situation in which Miss Ray shewn, during the last seventeen years, her first onset in life is involved in an obscurity, from which our most diligent enquiry has been able to collect but very few authentic particulars*. The distinc-

to marry him, she however framed various delays, and at length renounced all correspondence with him. SAGITTA alternately used complaints and menaces; adjuring her by the reputation which for her he had shipwrecked, by the wealth which upon her he had totally consumed; lastly, he told her, that his life and person was the only fortune left him, and of that too the disposal lay wholly in her breast. At length, perceiving her deaf to all his reasonings, he requested the consolation of one parting night; for that thus calmed and gratified, he would thenceforth be able to govern his passion. The night was granted and named, and PONTIA appointed a maid her confidante to secure the chamber. SAGITTA brought with him one freedman, and a dagger concealed under his robe. The interview began, as usual, in combinations of love and anger, with a medley of chiding and beseeching, of reproaches and submission; and part too of the night was devoted to joy and embraces: at last he became enraged with expostulations and despair, and suddenly plunged his dagger into her heart...— [*Tacitus' Annals, lib. xiii.*

Nullæ sunt inimicitæ nisi amoris acerbæ. PROPERT.

No enmities so bitter as those which proceed from love.

—— "It is," says MONTAIGNE, "a furious agitation "that throws them back to an extremity quite contrary to "its cause."

* If probable conjecture can be admitted to supply the deficiency of authentic information, it may certainly be made use of in writing the memoirs of a modern courtezan: their lives are generally

distinctions of family or fortune, so essential to those who would rank in the circles of the great and fashionable world, shed not their lustre on the humble sphere of life in which Miss Ray originally moved; but these adventitious aids, liberal nature amply supplied, by a profusion of her more rare and estimable gifts: the character left us by Sallust of the beautiful, the gay, and accomplished Sempronia, was pe-

generally uniform, however as individuals, they may differ in point of situation, or personal attractions: pleasure and interest are the ultimate objects of their views, and their occupations. But the causes which lead them to swerve from those principles of virtue, which constitute their sex's noblest boast, and brightest ornament, often vary. And first, those who possess that degree of sentiment, sensibility, and delicacy of thinking, which, without a portion of prudence sufficient to direct them in their intercourse with the world, often proves subversive of the virtue, and destructive to the happiness of their owner. These, tho' they are the most estimable, are too the most amiably weak principles of our nature; and men skilled in the arts of seduction, who, Proteus like, can assume the semblance of vice, or virtue, at will; find a peculiar facility in making these qualities the ready instruments to effect the ruin of their possessor. Over such amiable victims, virtue mourns, and sympathy pays the tribute of a tear, to the lamentable fate of sensibility and beauty.

In the second rank may be classed those, who, with perhaps, an equal share of beauty, have hearts which are less susceptible of tender impressions: such form an early and a just estimate of the world; as well as of their own qualities and endowments; acquire the art of displaying these to advantage, by attention to, and a dextrous management of the passions, and foibles of their admirers. Among the latter we shall place Miss Ray.

culiarly applicable to Miſs Ray. ‘ She was beautiful, excelled in muſic, ſinging, and dancing, with language at her command, ſhe could ſuit it to any occaſion ; was modeſt, alluring, and wanton in it, by turns; and to ſum up all, ſhe had the readieſt conception, and a fund of vivacity never to be exhauſted.’

Miſs Martha Ray was born in the year 1746. Her father, Mr. Jonathan Ray, was formerly a woollen-draper, in Taviſtoc-court, Covent-garden, London. But his failure in trade, (the conſequence, it is ſaid, of Mr. Ray's too great propenſity to pleaſurable purſuits,) taking place, he did not long ſurvive the miſfortune: the proſpect of impending poverty, and the poignant reflection of having reduced from a ſtate of affluence and independence, to want and diſtreſs, an amiable wife and family, contributed to haſten his death ; ſoon after which Mrs. Ray, with her two daughters, (of whom Miſs Martha Ray is ſaid to have been the youngeſt,) retired to obſcure lodgings in Clerkenwell ; where they continued to reſide for a number of years. Mrs. Ray followed the profeſſion of a mantua-maker.

During Miſs Ray's reſidence at Covent-garden, ſhe had conſtantly attended the amuſements of the theatre: to her lively fancy, it then preſented peculiar alurements, and ſhe contracted a predilection for it, which ſhe ever after retained. At length, motives of neceſſity, as well as inclination, induced her to embrace a theatrical life ; and ſhe was ſcarcely ſixteen, at her firſt appearance as a public ſinger, on

Covent-

Covent-garden theatre. Tho' young, she already displayed charms, which indicated — beauty ripening into perfection: her person was engaging, and her voice flexible, full, and harmonious; all contributed to the eclat with which her first performance was received; the connoisseurs in beauty, and the critical judges of vocal excellence, were equally unanimous, and flattering, in the praise which they bestowed, and the future excellence which they announced.

In a situation so conspicuous, she soon became the object of general attention; and every day encreased the number of her admirers: (many of whom were professed suitors), among these, Mr. Hackman was distinguished by Miss Ray with peculiar marks of esteem. Mr. Hackman to a fine person, added those captivating graces of address, and conversation; which form an irresistible union, and which rarely fail of making the powerful and favourable impression on a female heart. No wonder then, that whilst motives of mere interest induced Miss Ray to engage in amours with several, who, in rank and fortune, were superior to Mr. Hackman, that he, only should boast of the united possession of her heart and person.

Their connection continued for three years, in an uninterrupted flow of reciprocal enjoyment. Time, that 'clips the wings of love,' perceived no abatement in Mr. Hackman's affections, he doated on Miss Ray to a degree that bordered on an enthusiastick attach-

attachment: but wishing at once, by the most honourable of ties, to crown and cement his happiness; he repeatedly proposed marriage to her, which she constantly rejected; perhaps like Eloisa, (or the celebrated Miss C——. a lady, who, in our days, has adopted the same doctrine, but with better fortune), she held that,

> '*Love, free as air, at sight of human ties,*
> '*Spreads his light wings, and in a moment flies.*' POPE.

But motives more prudential were assigned by Miss Ray; a tie of children * by a noble lord, high in office, put a bar to their union, and she was determined, in opposition to the most pressing intreaties from Mr. Hackman, to decline matrimony. He being at this time an officer in the army, and necessarily compelled to leave her at times, her absence was of too painful a nature for an affection like his to sustain with fortitude: he again renewed his solicitations to Miss Ray, on the subject, but with no better success than before.

At the commencement of Miss Ray's connection with Lord S——, she is said to have informed his lordship of her prior acquaintance with Mr. Hackman, and of his situation in life; and interested herself so effectually in Mr. Hackman's favour, that she obtained from his lordship a promise of promoting in

* Miss Ray had five children by his lordship, one of which, a fine youth of sixteen, is now a lieutenant in the navy; and served under Sir Hugh Palliser, in the Formidable, during the action of the 27th July last.

the

the utmost extent, Mr. Hackman's advancement in the church†, which, however opposite to the military profession

† The influence of Miss Ray over her noble keeper was extreme; and it is said, that many who now possess lucrative and honourable posts, in the ecclesiastical, civil, and military departments, are indepted to her mediation for their advancement. It has even been asserted, but with what degree of truth we shall not pretend to determine, that secrets of S— were not reserved from this confidential favourite.—See the 'Political Duenna,' published a few months since; the satyrical author of which, under the name of Clara Raymond, first introduced her history to the world: the reader may form, from the following scene, no incomplete idea of the unfortunate lady's domestic character, and conduct, as well as that of her fond Limberham.

Enter Twitcher.

Well,—this girl is the plague of my life,—my punishment by day, and my torment by night.—Yet, spight of age, and impotence, I love her,—and—

Song. Tune.—By him we love offended.

When those we love enrage us,
How soon our passion flies!
The slut can re-engage us,
And kill us with her eyes!

Last night, the little gipsy
I bid depart my house;
She told me I was tipsey,
Nor valued me a souse.

Yet, were she now to enter,
And catch me in this place:
I fear I scarce could venture,
To look upon her face.
When those we love, &c.

The

profession, was considered by the latter as the ... eligible line he could eggage in; and as present...

The little, artful baggage,
  Has often said she lov'd;
And tho' next hour she wrong'd me,
  I told her I approv'd.

That all she did was charming,
  So long as she was kind;
When with a song she pays me,
  Her faults are thrown behind.

Enter Clara Raymond.

Clara. Where is this tyrant keeper of mine? this lord of anchors and cables? this emperor of the dock yards?—O! are you there?—You sneaking, pimping, incapable—Oh! I could tear your eyes out, you old goat! you a peer! — you are nothing but the pander of your own vices; like Chartres, you have long deserved the gallows, for what you have done, and what you cannot do.

Twitcher. Soft, my Clara,—softly, I beseech thee,—a piano note, my lovely girl. Thou knowest I cannot bear that thundering sound.—Come, Clara, buss and be friends.—Sing me a song, you little devil.

Clara. Not I truly,—I'll neither kiss nor sing. (peevishly.

Twitcher. Indeed but you must, my Clara.

Clara. Buy me the diamond necklace then.

Twit. I would, if I could spare cash;—but upon my honour—

Clara. O! curse your honour,—I'll have none on't.—The necklace, Sir, or the ready money,—or I'm off,—positively off. Why I was better off when I was a mantua maker in Clerkenwell, than I am with you, cruel and unkind that you are.—(weeps.

Twitcher. Nay, my lovely girl, I cannot bear those tears,—here,—here,—take this bill for a hundred; and thou shalt have

the

the greatest probability of speedy preferment. Shortly after, he quit the military habit, and assumed that of

the remainder to-morrow: damn it, what signifies mincing the matter,—I must squeeze the chest at Chatham.

SONG. Tune,—How oft, Louisa, &c.

How oft, my Clara, hast thou said,
(The fondness of thy heart to prove,)
That Twitcher was thy dearest friend,
Nor would'st thou seek another love.

And by those lips that sweetly swore,
And by those eyes that shine so bright,
I ne'er lov'd woman so before,
For Clara is my soul's delight.

Then let me press those ruby lips,
And on that lovely breast repose,
Exhaling fragrance from thy breath;
Fragrance that far excels the rose.

Thus let us spend the livelong day,
And thus the tedious nights beguile;
The cares of state I shall not feel,
So Clara sing, and Clara smile!

Clara. Why, aye, this is something like breeding; a complimentary song, and a hundred guineas: but I must have the rest to-morrow.

Twitcher. Positively.—But give me one song, my charmer.

Clara. I believe I have a little piece you have not yet heard, and you are such a bewithing devil there is no refusing you any thing.

SONG. Tune.—Adieu thou dreary pile.

Farewel all angry thoughts, for Twitcher loves,
And by the solid gold his passion proves!

At

of the canonical; it may, however, be obſerved, th no reſolutions of celibacy, no ſentiments of morti cation, accompanied or dictated the tranſition; t violent paſſions of the lover, and thoſe objects whi conſtitute the purſuit of a man of the world, ſtill tained their aſcendency.

Mr. Hackman ſtill continued to ſolicit Miſs R to agree to their marriage; ſhe, at length, weari out by theſe importunities, is ſaid to have wit drawn herſelf wholly from him. This reſo tion Miſs Ray had adhered to, for upwards of fi years, during which time Mr. Hackman, with all ardour and ſolicitous importunity of the moſt paſſi ate lover, was conſtant in his applications to M Ray, both in perſon and by letter: this is ſaid have produced a meeting very lately between the the conſequence of which was a quarrel, and forbidding him ever to apply to, or think of more; ſhe then took a final leave of him.

> At home, your virtuous fools may moaping ſtay;
> Give me the ball, the opera, and the play!
> Cornely's groves, which fan each ſoft deſire,
> —— —— —— —— ——

And ſo, your ſervant, my lord; I'm engag'd to-night w private party. [Exit Clara

Twitcher, ſolus.

Enchanting devil!—This girl would be the utter ruin of at ſeventy years of age, if my fortune was not already diſſip and my character loſt beyond recovery.—But I muſt now t fineſs; and try how to raiſe a ſum, by advancing ſome wort ſcoundrel over the head of a hundred men of merit.

END OF THE MEMOIRS.

LOVE

AND

MADNESS, &c.

LETTER I.

To Miss ——.

Huntingdon, Dec. 4, 1774.

Dear M.

TEN thousand thanks for your billet by my corporal Trim yesterday. The fellow seemed happy to have been the bearer of it, because he saw it made *me* happy. He will be as good a soldier to Cupid as to Mars, I dare say. And Mars and Cupid are not now to begin their acquaintance, you know.

 Whichever

Whichever he ſerves, you may command him of courſe, without a compliment; for Venus, I need not tell *you*, is the mother of Cupid, and miſtreſs of Mars.

At preſent the drum is beating up under my window for volunteers to Bacchus—In plain Engliſh, the drum tells me dinner is ready; for a drum gives us bloody-minded heroes an appetite for eating, as well as for fighting; nay we get up by the beat of it, and it every night ſends, or ought to ſend us, to bed and to ſleep. To-night it will be late before I get to one or the other, I fancy—indeed, the thoughts of you would prevent the latter. But, the next diſgrace to refuſing a challenge, is refuſing a toaſt. The merit of a jolly fellow and of a ſpunge is much about the ſame. For my part, no glaſs of any liquor taſtes as it ſhould to me, but when I kiſs my M. on the rim.

Adieu—Whatever hard ſervice I may have after dinner, no quantity of wine ſhall make me yet drop or forget my appointment with you to-morrow. We certainly

were

were not ſeen yeſterday, for reaſons I will give you.

Though you ſhould perſiſt in never being mine,

Ever, ever

Your's.

LETTER II.

To the Same.

Huntingdon, Dec. 6, 1775.

My deareſt M.

No—I will not take advantage of the ſweet, reluctant, amorous confeſſion which your candour gave me yeſterday. If to make me happy be to make my M. otherwiſe; then, happineſs, I'll none of thee.

And yet I *could* argue. Suppoſe he *has* bred you up——Suppoſe you *do* owe your numerous accompliſhments, under genius, to him——are you therefore his property? Is it as if a horſe that he has bred up ſhould refuſe to carry him? Suppoſe you therefore *are* his property——Will the fidelity of many years weigh nothing in the ſcale of gratitude?

Years——why, can obligations (ſuppoſe they had *not* been repaid an hundred fold) do away the unnatural diſparity of years? Can they bid five-and-fifty ſtand ſtill (the leaſt that you could aſk), and wait for five-and twenty? Many women have the ſame obligations (if indeed there be many of the *ſame* accompliſhments) to their fathers. They have the additional obligation to them (if, indeed, it be an obligation) of exiſtence. The diſparity of years is ſometimes even leſs. —But, muſt they therefore take their fathers to their boſoms? Muſt the jeſſamine fling its tender arms around the dying elm?

To my little fortunes you are no ſtranger. Will you ſhare them with me? And you ſhall honeſtly tell his lordſhip that gratitude taught you to pay every duty to him, till love taught you there were other duties which you owed to H.

Gracious

Gracious Heaven that you *would* pay them!

But did I not ſay I would not take advantage? I will not. I will even remind you of your children; to whom I, alas, could only ſhew at preſent the *affection* of a father.

M. weigh us in the ſcales. If gratitude out-balance love—ſo.

If you command it, I ſwear by love, I'll join my regiment to-morrow.

If love prevail, and inſiſt upon his dues; you ſhall declare the victory and the prize. I *will* take no advantage.

Think over this. Neither will I take you by ſurprize. *Sleep upon it*, before you return your anſwer. Trim ſhall make the old excuſe to-morrow. And, thank Heaven! to-night you ſleep alone.

Why did you ſing that ſweet ſong yeſterday, though I ſo preſſed you? Thoſe words and your voice, were too much.

No words can ſay how much I am your's.

LETTER III.

To Mr. ——.

H.
Dec. 7, 1775.

My dear H.

HERE has been a ſad piece of work ever ſince I received your's yeſterday. But, don't be alarmed—We are not diſcovered to the prophane. Our tender tale is only known to—(whom does your fear ſuggeſt ?)—to love and gratitude, my H. And they ought both for twenty reaſons, to be *your* friends, I am ſure.

They have been trying your cauſe, ever ſince the departure of honeſt Trim yeſterday. Love, though in my opinion not ſo blind, is as good a juſtice, as Sir John Fielding. I argued the matter ſtoutly—my head on his lordſhip's ſide of the queſtion, my heart on your's. At laſt they ſeemed to ſay, as if the oath of allegiance, which I had taken to gratitude, at a time when, Heaven knows, I had never heard of love, ſhould

ſhould be void, and I ſhould be at full liberty to devote myſelf, body and ſoul, to —But call on me to-morrow before dinner, and I'll tell you their final Judgment. This I will tell you now—love ſent you the tendereſt wiſhes, and gratitude ſaid I could never pay you all I owe you for your noble letter of yeſterday. . . . . .

Yet—oh, my H. think not meanly of me ever for this——Do not you turn advocate againſt me——I will not pain you ——'tis impoſſible you ever ſhould.

Come then to-morrow—and ſurely Omiah will not murder love! Yet I thought the other day he caught our eyes converſing. Eyes ſpeak a language all can underſtand. ——But, is a child of nature to nip in the bud that favourite paſſion which his mother Nature planted, and ſtill tends?—What will Oberea and her coterie ſay to this, Omiah, when you return from making the tour of the globe? They'll black-ball you, depend on it.

What would Rouſſeau ſay to it, my H.?

You ſhall tell me to-morrow. I will

not write another word; lest conſcience, who is juſt now looking over my left ſhoulder, ſhould ſnatch my pen, and ſcratch out *to-morrow*.

LETTER IV.

To Miſs ——.

Huntingdon, Dec. 7, 1775.

My deareſt Soul,

I HOPE to Heaven Trim will be able to get this to you to-night!—Not I only, but my whole future life, ſhall thank you for the dear ſheet of paper I have juſt received. Bleſſings, bleſſings—But I could write and exclaim, and offer up vows and prayers, till the happy hour arrives.

Yet, hear me, M. If I have thus far deſerved your love, I will deſerve it ſtill. As a proof I have not hitherto preſſed you for any thing conſcience diſapproves, you ſhall not do to-morrow what conſcience diſapproves. You ſhall not make me happy (oh, how ſupremely bleſt!) under the roof

of

of your benefactor and my host. It were not honourable. Our love, the inexorable tyrant of our hearts, claims his sacrifice; but does not bid us insult his Lordship's walls with it. How civilly did he invite me to H. in October last, though an unknown recruiting officer! How politely himself first introduced me to himself! Often has the recollection made me struggle with my passion. Still it shall restrain it on this side honour.

So far from triumphing or exulting, Heaven knows——if Lord S. indeed love you, if indeed it be aught beside the natural preference which age gives to youth——Heaven knows how much I pity him. Yet, as I have either said or written before, it is only the pity I should feel for a father whose affections were unfortunately and unnaturally fixed upon his own daughter.

Were I your seducer, M. and not your lover, I should not write thus—nor should I have talked or acted or written as I have. Tell it not in Gath, nor publish it in the streets of Askalon, lest the Philistines should be upon me. I ſhould be drummed out of my regiment for a traitor to intrigue. And can you really imagine I think ſo meanly of your ſex! Surely you cannot imagine I think ſo meanly of you. Why, then, the concluſion of your laſt letter but one? A word thereon.

Take men and women in the lump, the villainy of thoſe and the weakneſs of theſe —I maintain it to be leſs wonderful that an hundred or ſo ſhould fall in the world, than that even one ſhould ſtand. Is it ſtrange the ſerpent conquered Eve? The devil againſt a woman is fearful odds. He has conquered men, womens' conquerors; he he has made even angels fall.

Oh, then, ye parents, be merciful in your wrath. Join not the baſe betrayers of your children—drive not your children to the bottom of the precipice, becauſe the villains have driven them half way down, where (ſee, ſee!) many have ſtopped themſelves from falling further by catching hold of ſome ſtraggling virtue or another which decks the ſteep-down rock. Oh, do not force their weak hands from their hold—their laſt, laſt hold! The deſcent from crime to crime is natural, perpendicular, headlong enough, of itſelf—do not increaſe it.

" Can women, then, no way but backward fall?"

Shall I aſk your pardon for all this, M.? No, there is no occaſion, you ſay.

But to-morrow—for *to-morrow* led me out of my ſtrait path, over this fearful precipice, where I, for my part, trembled at every ſtep I took, leſt I ſhould topple down headlong. Glad am I to be once more on *plain* ground again with my M.!

To-morrow, about eleven, I'll be with you—but, let me find you in your riding dreſs, and your mare ready. I have laid a plan, to which neither honour nor delicacy (and I always conſult both before I propoſe any thing to *you*) can make the leaſt objection. This once, truſt to me—I'll explain all to-morrow. Pray be ready, in your *riding-dreſs!* Need I add, in that you know

I think

I think becomes you moſt? No—Love would have whiſpered that.

Love ſhall be of our party—He ſhall not ſuffer the cold to approach you—he ſhall ſpread his wings over your boſom—he ſhall neſtle in your dear arms—he ſhall—

When will to-morrow come? What torturing dreams muſt I not bear to-night!

I ſend you ſome lines which I picked up ſomewhere—I forget where. But I don't think them much amiſs.

CELIA's PICTURE.

To paint my Celia, I'd deviſe
Two ſummer ſuns, in place of eyes;
Two lunar orbs ſhould then be laid
Upon the boſom of the maid;
Bright Berenice's auburn hair
Should, where it ought, adorn my fair;
Nay all the ſigns in heaven ſhould prove
But tokens of my wondrous love.
All, did I ſay? Yes, all, ſave one——
Her yielding waiſt ſhould want a Zone.

LETTER V.

To the Same.

Huntingdon, 8th Dec. 1775.

THEN I releafe my deareft foul from her promife about to-day. If you do not fee that all which *he* can claim by gratitude, I doubly claim by love; I have done, and will for ever have done. I would purchafe my happinefs at any price but at the expence of your's.

Look over my letters, think over my conduct, confult your own heart, and read thefe two long letters of your writing, which I return you. Then, tell me whether we love or not. And—if we love (as witnefs both our hearts)—fhall gratitude, *cold* gratitude, bear away the heavenly prize that's only due to love like our's? fhall my right be acknowledged, and muft he poffefs the cafket? Shall I have your foul, and fhall he have your hand, your eyes, your bofom, your lips, your—

Gracious

Gracious God of Love! I can neither write, nor think. Send one line, half a line, to

your own, own

H.

LETTER VI.

To Mr. H——.

H. 10 Dec. 75.

YOUR two letters of the day before yeſterday, and what you ſaid to me yeſterday in my dreſſing-room, have drove me mad. To offer to ſell out, and take the other ſtep to get money for us both, was not kind. You know how ſuch tenderneſs diſtracts me. As to marrying me, that you ſhould not do upon any account. Shall the man I value be pointed at and hooted for ſelling himſelf to a Lord, for a commiſſion, or ſome ſuch thing, to marry his caſt miſtreſs? My ſoul is above my ſituation.—Beſides, I will not take advantage, Mr. H., of what may be only perhaps (excuſe me)

a youth-a youthful paſſion. After a more intimate acquaintance with me of a week or ten days, your opinion of me might very much change. And yet—you may love *me* as ſincerely as I—

But I will tranſcribe you a ſong which I don't believe you ever heard me ſing, though it's my favourite. It is ſaid to be an old Scots ballad——nor is it generally known that Lady A. L. wrote it. Since we have underſtood each other, I never ſung it before you, becauſe it is ſo deſcriptive of our ſituation——how much more ſo ſince your cruelly kind propoſal of yeſterday! I wept, like an infant, over it this morning.

AULD ROBIN GRAY.

The ſheep were in the fold, and the cows were all
 at home,
And all the weary world to reſt was gone,
When the woes of my heart brought the tear in
 mine e'e,
While my good man lay ſound by me.

Young Jamie lov'd me well, and he sought me for his bride,
He had but a crown, he had no more beside;
To make the crown a pound, young Jamie went to sea,
And the crown and the pound, they were both for me.

He had na been gone but a year and a day,
When my father broke his arm, and our cow was stole away;
When my mother she fell sick, and my Jamie at the sea,
And Auld Robin Gray came wooing to me.

My father could na work, and my mother could na spin,
I toiled night and day, but their bread I could na win;
Auld Rob maintained them both, and with tears in his e'e,
Said, " Jenny for their sakes, oh! marry me."

My heart it said no, and I wish'd for Jamie back,
But the wind it blew sore, and his ship it prov'd a wreck;
His ship prov'd a wreck: ah! why did not Jenny dee?
Why was she left to cry—" Ah, woe is me!"

My

My father argu'd ſore; though my mother did na ſpeak;
She look'd in my face till my heart was fit to break;
So auld Robin got my hand——but my heart was in the ſea,
——— And now Robin Gray is goodman to me.

I had na been a wife but of weeks only four,
When ſitting right mournfully out at my door,
I ſaw my Jamie's ghoſt, for I could na think 'twas he,
Till he ſaid, "Jenny, I'm come home to marry thee."

Sore did we weep, and little did we ſay,
We took but one kiſs—and we tore ourſelves away;
I wiſh I was dead, but I am not like to dee,
And oh! I am young to cry—"Ah, woe is me!"

I gang like a ghoſt, and I do not care to ſpin,
I fain would think on Jamie, but that would be a ſin;
I muſt e'en do my beſt a good wife to be,
For auld Robin Gray has been kind to me.

My poor eyes will only ſuffer me to add, for God's ſake, let me ſeee my *Jamie* to-moriow. Your name alſo is Jamie.

LET-

LETTER VII.

To Miſs ——.

Huntingdon,
13 Dec. 75.

My life and ſoul!

But I will never more uſe any preface of this ſort—And I beg you will not. A correſpondence begins with dear, then my dear, deareſt, my deareſt, and ſo on, 'till, at laſt, panting language toils after us in vain.

No language can explain my feelings. Oh M. yeſterday, yeſterday! Language, thou lieſt—there is no ſuch word as *ſatiety*, poſitively no ſuch word.——Oh, thou beyond my warmeſt dreams bewitching! what charms! what—

But words would poorly paint our joys. When, when?—yet you ſhall order, govern every thing. Only remember, I am *ſure* of thoſe we truſt.

Are you now convinced that Heaven made us for each other? By that Heaven,

by

by the paradise of your dear arms, I will be only yours!

Have I written sense? I know not what I write. This scrap of paper ('tis all I can find) will hold a line or two more. I must fill i up to say that, whatever evils envious fate design me, after those few hours of yesterday, I never will complain nor murmur.

Misfortune, I defy thee now.—M. loves me, and H,'s soul has its content most absolute. No other joy like this succeeds in unknown fate.

LETTER VIII.

To the Same.

Huntingdon,
24 Dec. 1775.

TALK not to me of the new year. I am a new man. I'll be sworn to it I am not the same identical J. H. that I was three months ago. You have created me—yes, I know what I say—created me anew.

As to thanking you for the bliss I taste with

with you—to attempt it would be id What thanks can expreſs the heaven heavens——

But I will obey you in not giving ſuch looſe to my pen as I gave the day befo yeſterday. That letter and the verſes contained, which were certainly too highly coloured, pray commit to the flames. Yet, pray too, as I begged you yeſterday, do not imagine I thought leſs chaſtely of you becauſe I wrote them. By Heaven, I believe your mind as chaſte as the ſnow which, while I write, is driving againſt my window. You know not *what* I think of you. One time perhaps you may.

The lines I repeated to you this morning, I ſend you. Upon my honour they are not mine. I think of them quite as you do. Surely an additional merit in them is, that to the uninitiated, in whom they might perhaps raiſe improper ideas, they are *totally unintelligible*.

LET-

LETTER IX.

To Mr. ——.

H.
Chriſtmas-day, 75.

My old friend the Corporal looked as if he had been tarred and feathered yeſterday, when he arrived with your *dear* billet. Omiah took up the ſugar-caſter, when he ſaw him through the parlour window, and powdered a freſh ſlice of pudding, by way of *painting* the ſnowy Corporal. Omiah's ſimplicity is certainly very diverting, but I ſhould like him better, and take more pains with him, if I did not think he ſuſpected ſomething. The other day, I am ſure he came to ſpy the nakedneſs of the land. Thank Heaven, our caution prevented him.

But, why do I call your billet *dear*, when it contained ſuch poetry? Yet, to confeſs the truth, it *did* charm me. And I know not, whether as you ſay, thoſe, to whom it could do any harm, could poſſibly underſtand it. For *uninitiated* means, I believe, not yet admitted into the myſteries—thoſe who have not yet taken the veil; or, *I* ſhould rather ſay, thoſe who have not yet thrown off the veil. Why was I not permitted by my deſtiny to keep on mine, till my H. my *Mars ſeized me in his ardent arms?* How gladly to *his* arms would I have given up my very ſoul!

Cruel fortune, that it can't be ſo to-day! But we forgot when we fixed on to-day, that it would be Chriſtmas-day. I muſt do penance at a moſt *unpleaſant* dinner, as indeed is every meal and every ſcene when you are abſent—and that, without the conſolation of having firſt enjoyed your company. To-morrow, however, at the uſual time and place. Your diſcontinuing your viſits here, ſince the firſt day of our happineſs, gratifies the delicacy of us both. Yet, may it not, my H., raiſe ſuſpicions elſewhere? Your agreeable qualities were too conſpicuous not to make you miſſed. Yet, *you* are the beſt judge.

My poor, innocent, helpleſs babes! Were it not on your account, your mother

would

would not *act* the part ſhe does.—What is Mrs. Yates's ſuſtaining a character well for one evening? Is it ſo trying as to play a part, and a baſe one too, morning, noon, and night?—*Night!* But I will not make my H. uneaſy.

At leaſt, allow that I have written you a long ſcrawl. Behold, I have ſent you a tolerable good ſubſtitute for myſelf. It is reckoned very like. I need not beg you not to ſhew it. Only remember, the painter's M. is not to rob your own M. of a certain quantity of things called and known by the name of k ſſes, which I humbly conceive to be her due, though ſhe has been diſappointed of them to-day.

So, having nothing further to add at preſent, and the poſt being juſt going out, I remain with all truth,

Dear Sir,

Your moſt humble ſervant,

M.

There's

There's a pretty conclusion for you. Am I not a good girl? I shall become a most elegant correspondent in time, I see. This paragraph is the postscript, you know— and should therefore have been introduced by a well flourished P. S. the Sir Clement Cottrel upon these occasions.

LETTER X.

To Miss ——.

Huntingdon,
28 Dec. 75.

Your condescension in removing my most *groundless* cause of jealousy yesterday, was more than I deserved. How I exposed myself by my violence with you! But, I tell you my passions are all gunpowder. Though, thank God, no Othello, yet am I

"One not easily jealous; but, being wrought,
"Perplex'd in th' extreme;"

And that God knows how I love you, worship you, idolize you.

How

How *could* I think you particular to ſuch a thing as B? You ſaid you forgave me to-day, and I hope you did. Let me have it again from your own dear lips to-morrow, inſtead of the next day. Every thing ſhall be ready—and the guitar, which I wrote for, is come down, and I'll bring the ſong and you ſhall ſing it, and play it, and I'll beg you to forgive me, and you ſhall forgive me, and,—five hundred ands beſides.

Why, I would be jealous of this ſheet of paper, if you kiſſed it with too much rapture.

What a fool!—No, my M., rather ſay—what a lover!

Many thanks for your picture. It *is* like. Accept this proof that I have examined it.

'Tis true, creative man, thine art can teach
The living picture every thing but ſpeech!—
True, thou haſt drawn her, as ſhe is, all fair,
Divinely fair! her lips, her eyes, her hair!

Full well I know the ſmile upon that face
Full well I know thoſe features' eve
grace!
But what is this—my M.'s mortal part—
There *is* a ſubject beggars all thine art:
Paint but her *mind*, by Heav'n! and th
ſhalt be,
Shalt be my more than pagan deity.—
Nature may poſſibly have caſt, of *old*,
Some other beauty in as fair a mould—
But all in vain you'll ſearch the world
find
Another beauty with ſo fair a mind.

LETTER XI.

To the Same.

Huntingdon, 1 Jan. 17

LEST I ſhould not ſee you this mornin I will ſcribble this before I mount hon Crop; that I may leave it for you.

This is a new year. May every day it be happy to my M. May—but dor you know there's not a wiſh of bliſs I do not wiſh you?

A *new* year—I like not this world. There may be new lovers.—I lie—there may not. M. will never change her H. I am ſure ſhe'll never change him for a truer lover.

A new year—76. Where ſhall we be in 77? Where in 78? Where in 79? Where in 80?

In miſery or bliſs, in life or death, in heaven or hell—wherever *you* are there may H. be alſo!

The ſoldier whom you deſired me to beg off, returns thanks to his unknown benefactreſs.—Diſcipline muſt be kept up in our way; but I am ſure you will do me the juſtice to believe I am no otherwiſe a friend to it.

LETTER XII.

To the Same.

Huntingdon, Feb. 8, 1776.

SINCE the thaw ſent me from H. the day before yeſterday, I have written four times to you, and believe verily I ſhall write four-and-forty times to you in the next four days. The bliſs I have enjoyed with you theſe three weeks has increaſed, not diminiſhed, my affection. Three weeks and more in the ſame houſe with my M.!—'Twas more than I deſerved. And yet, to be obliged to reſign you every night to another!—By theſe eyes, by your ſtill dearer eyes, I don't think I ſlept three hours during the whole three weeks. Yet, yet, *'twas* bliſs. How lucky, that I was preſſed to ſtay at H. the night the ſnow ſet in! Would it had ſnowed till doomſday! But, then, you muſt have been *his* every night till doomſday. Now, my happy time may come.

Though

Though I had not ſtrength to reſiſt when under the ſame roof with you, ever ſince we parted, the recollection that it was *his* roof has made me miſerable. Whimſical, that he ſhould bid *you* preſs me, when I at firſt refuſed his ſolicitation.—Is H. guilty of a breach of hoſpitality?

I muſt not queſtion—I muſt not think, I muſt not write.—But, we will meet as we fixed.

Does Robin Gray ſuſpect?—Suſpect! And is H. a ſubject for ſuſpicion?

LETTER XIII.

To the Same.

Huntingdon, 16 Feb. 1776.

EVERY time I ſee you I diſcover ſome new charm, ſome new accompliſhment. Before Heaven, there was not a tittle of flattery in what I told you yeſterday. Nothing *can* be flattery which I ſay of you, for no invention, no poetry, no any thing can come up to what I *think* of you.

One of our Kings ſaid of the citizens of his good city of London, that when he conſidered their riches, he was in admiration at their underſtandings—when he conſidered their underſtandings, he was in admiration at their riches. Juſt ſo do I with regard to your perſon and your mind, but for a different reaſon.—Nature was in one of her extravagant moods when ſhe put you together. She might have made two captivating women out of you—by my ſoul, half a dozen! Your turn for muſic, and excellence in it, would be a ſufficient ſtock of charms for the moſt diſagreeable woman to ſet up with in life. Muſic has charms to do things moſt incredible, muſic—

Now ſhall I, with the good-humoured, digreſſive pen of our favourite Montaigne in his entertaining Eſſays, begin with love, and end with a treatiſe upon the Gamut.

Yet to talk of muſic, is to talk of you. M. and muſic are the ſame. What is muſic

without

without you? And harmony has turned your mind, your perſon, your every look, and word, and action.

Obſerve—when I write to you I never pretend to write ſenſe. I have no head; you have made me all heart, from top to bottom. Senſe—why, I am out of my ſenſes, and have been theſe ſix weeks. Were it poſſible my ſcrawls to you could ever be read by any one but you, I ſhould be called a madman. I certainly am either curſt or bleſt (I know not which) with paſſions wild as the torrent's roar. Notwithſtanding I take this ſimile from water, the element out of which I am formed, is fire. Swift had water in his brain: I have a burning coal of fire: your hand can light it up to rapture, rage, or madneſs. Men, real men, have never been wild enough for my admiration: it has wandered into the ideal world of fancy. Othello (but he ſhould have put *himſelf* to death in his wife's ſi ght, *not* his wife), Zanga, are *my heroes.* Milk-and-water paſſions are like ſentimental comedy. Give me (you ſee, how, like your friend Montaigne, I ſtrip myſelf of my ſkin, and ſhew you all my veins and arteries even the playing of my heart) ——give *me*, I ſay, tragedy, affecting tragedy, in the world, as well as in the theatre.—— I would maſſacre all mankind ſooner than loſe you.——

——This is mere madneſs;
And thus, a while. the fit will work on
 him;
Anon, as patient as the female dove
When that her golden couplets are diſ-
 cloſed,
His ſilence will ſit drooping.

Inconſiſtent being! While I am ranting thus about tragedy, and blood, and murder —behold, I am as weak as a woman. My tears flow at but the idea of loſing you. Yes, they don't drop only; they pour; I ſob, like a child. Is this Othello, is this Zanga? We know not what we are, nor what we may become.

This

This I know, that I am and ever will be your's and only your's.

I ſend you Oſſian. You will ſee what a favourite he is with me, by ſome drawings, and pieces of (what your partiality will call) poetry, which accompany the bard of other times. Should you quit this world before me, which fate forbid, often ſhall I hear your ſpirit (if I can be weak enough to ſurvive you) calling me from the low-ſailing cloud of night.—They abuſe Macpherſon for calling them tranſlations. If he alone be the author of them, why does he not ſay ſo, and claim the prize of fame; I proteſt *I* would. They who do not refuſe their admiration to the compoſitions, ſtill think themſelves juſtified to abuſe Macpherſon, for pretending *not* to be the author of what they ſtill admire. Is not this ſtrange?

As we could not meet this morning (how long muſt our meetings depend on others, and not on ourſelves?) I was determined, you ſee, to have a long converſation with you.

Pray ſeal, in future, with better wax, and more care. Something colder than one of my kiſſes might have thawed the ſeal of yeſterday. But I will not talk of *thawing*. Had the froſt and ſnow continued, I had ſtill been with you at H.

The remainder of this (my ſecond ſheet of paper, obſerve) ſhall be filled with what I think a valuable curioſity. The officer, whom you ſaw with me on Sunday, is lately come from America. He gave it me, and aſſures me it is original. It will explain itſelf. Would I might be in your dear, little, enchanted dreſſing-room, while you read it!

The Speech of a Shawaneſe Chief, to Lord Dunmore.

"I appeal to any white man to-day, if ever he entered Logan's cabin hungry, and he gave him not meat; if he ever came cold or naked, and I gave him not clothing. During

During the laſt long and bloody war, Logan remained idle, ignominious, in his cabin, an advocate for peace. Such was my love of the Whites, that thoſe of mine own country pointed at me as they paſſed by, and ſaid, "Logan is the friend of white men." I had even thought to live with you. But the injuries of one among you, did away that thought, and dragged me from my cabin of peace. Colonel Creſſop, the laſt ſpring, in cold blood, cut off all the relations of Logan, ſparing neither women nor children. There runs not a drop of the blood of Logan in the veins of any human creature. This calſed on me for revenge. I have ſought it. I have killed many. Revenge has been fully glutted.

"For my country—I rejoice at the beams of peace. But, harbour not the thought that mine is the joy of fear. Logan never felt fear. He will not turn his heel to ſave his life.

"Who is there to mourn for Logan?—Not one."

LET-

LETTER XIV.

To the Same.

Huntingdon, 22d Feb. 1776.

How ſilly we were, both of us, not to recollect your favourite Jenny? and did not Jamie think of her either?

——" Though my mother did na ſpeak,
She look'd in my face, till my heart was fit to break."

Was not this exactly the inſtance we wanted?

Something more has occurred to me on the ſame ſubject. Rather than not write to you, or than write to you as *deſcriptively* as recollection ſometimes tempts me, I know you would have me write nonſenſe.

In Hervey's "Meditations" are two paſſages as fine as they are ſimple and natural.

" A beam or two finds its way through
" the grates, and reflects a feeble glimmer
" from

" from the nails of the coffins."—" Should " the haggard ſkeleton lift a clattering hand—." In the latter, I know not whether the epithet *haggard* might not be ſpared.

Governor Holwell, in the account of the ſufferings at the black hole at Calcutta, when he ſpeaks of the length of time he ſupported nature by catching the drops, occaſioned by the heat, which fell from his head and face, adds theſe words—" You cannot imagine how unhappy I was when any one of them eſcaped my tongue!" What a ſcene! The happineſs, the exiſtence of a fellow creature, dependent upon being able to catch a drop of his own ſweat! Shakeſpeare's fancy could not have invented, nor ever did invent, any thing more ſublime; for this is nature, and nature itſelf is ſublimity.—People write *upon* a particular ſituation, they do not put themſelves *in* the ſituation. We only ſee the writer, ſitting in his ſtudy, and working up a ſtory to amuſe or to frighten; not the identical

identical Tom Jones, nor Macbeth himſelf.

Can you become the very being you deſcribe? Can you look round, and mark only that which ſtrikes in your new character, and forget all which ſtruck in your own? Can you bid your comfortable ſtudy, be the priſon of innocence or the houſe of mourning? Can you transform your garret of indigence into the palace of pleaſure? If you cannot, you had better clean ſhoes, than endeavour by writings to intereſt the imagination. We cannot even bear to ſee an author only peeping over the top of every page, to obſerve how we like him. The player I would call a corporal actor, the writer a mental actor. Garrick would in vain have put his face and his body in all the ſituations of Lear, if Shakeſpeare had not before put his mind in them all. In a thouſand inſtances, we have nothing to do but to copy nature, if we can only get her to ſit our pencil. And yet—how few of the

the moſt eminent maſters are happy enough to hit off her difficult face exactly!

Every perſon of taſte would have been certain that Mr. Holwell was one of the ſufferers in the black hole, only from the ſhort paſſage I have noticed.

Robinſon Cruſoe now—what nature! It affects us throughout, exactly in the way you mentioned.

But, ſhall I finiſh my diſſertation? Come —as writing to you gives me ſo much pleaſure, and as I can't do any thing to you but write this morning——I know you'll excuſe me.

Did you ever hear to what Cruſoe owed his exiſtence? You remember Alexander Selkirk's ſtrange ſequeſtration at Juan Fernandez. It is mentioned, I believe, in Walter's account of Anſon's Voyage. When Captain Woodes Rogers met with him and brought him to England, he employed the famous Daniel de Foe to reviſe his papers. That fertile genius improved upon his materials, and compoſed the celebrated

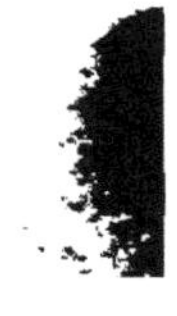

brated ſtory of Robinſon Cruſoe. The conſequence was that Selkirk, who ſoon after made his appearance in print, was conſidered as a baſtard of Cruſoe, with which ſpurious offspring the preſs too often teems. In De Foe, undoubtedly, this was not honeſt. Had Selkirk given him his papers, there could have been no harm in working them up his own way. I can eaſily conceive a writer making his own uſe of a known fact, and filling up the outlines which have been ſketched by the bold and haſty hand of fate. A moral may be added, by ſuch means, to a particular incident; characters may be placed in their juſt and proper lights; mankind may be amuſed, (and amuſements ſometimes prevent crimes) or, if the ſtory be criminal mankind may be bettered, through the channel of their curioſity. But, I would not be diſhoneſt, like De Foe; nor would I pain the breaſt of a ſingle individual connected with the ſtory.

To explain what I mean by a criminal ſtory.—Faldoni and Tereſa might have been prevented from making proſelytes, if they ever have made any, by working up their moſt affecting ſtory ſo as to take off the edge of the dangerous example. But not in the way Mr. Jerningham has done it; who tells us, not leſs intelligibly than pathetically,

All-ruling love, the god of youth poſſeſs'd
Entire dominion of Faldoni's breaſt:
An equal flame did ſymphany impart
(A flame deſtructive) to Tereſa's heart:
As on one ſtem two opening flowers re-
ſpire,
So grew their life (entwin'd) on one deſire.

Are you not charmed? Perhaps you never ſaw the poem. I have it here and will bring it you as a curioſity: the melancholy tale will not take up three words, though Mr. J. has beſtowed upon it 335 melancholy lines. The cataſtrophe happen'd near Lyons, in the month of June, 1770. Two lovers (Faldoni and Tereſa Meunier)

Meunier) meting with an invincible obſtacle to their union, determined to put an end to their exiſtence with piſtols. The place they choſe for the execution of their terrible project was a chapel that ſtood at a little diſtance from the houſe. They even decorated the altar for the occaſion. They paid a particular attention to their own dreſs. Tereſa was dreſſed in white, with roſe-coloured ribbands. The ſame coloured ribbands were tied to the piſtols. Each held the ribband that was faſtened to the other's trigger, which they drew at a certain ſignal.

Arria and Pætus (ſays Voltaire) ſet the example, but then it muſt be conſidered they were condemned to death by a tyrant. Whereas love was the only inventor and perpetrator of this deeed.

Yet, while I talk of taking off the dangerous edge of their example, they have almoſt liſted me under their bloody banners.—

On

On looking over the ſermon I have written, I recollect a curious anecdote of Selkirk.

(By the bye, Wilkes, I ſuppoſe, would ſay, that none but a Scotchman could have lived ſo many years upon a deſart iſland.)

He tamed a great number of kids for ſociety, and with them and the numerous offspring of two or three cats that had been left with him, he uſed often to dance.—From all which my inference is this—M. will not ſurely deprive herſelf of H's ſociety; but will let him find her *there* to-morrow. Eſpecially, ſince, in Mr. J.'s *expreſſive* language,

As on one ſtem two opening flowers
    reſpire,
So grow our lives entwin'd on one deſire.

LETTER

LETTER XV.

To Mr. ——.

H. 23 Feb. 76.

Where was you this morning, my life? I ſhould have been froze to death I believe with the cold, if I had not been waiting for *you*. I am uneaſy, very uneaſy. What could prevent you? Your own appointment too. Why not write, if you could not come?——Then I had a dream laſt night, a ſad dream, my H.

———"For thee I fear, my love;
Such ghaſtly dreams laſt night ſurprized my ſoul."

You may reply, perhaps, with my favourite Iphis,

Heed not theſe black illuſions of the night,
The mockings of unquiet ſlumbers."

Alas, I cannot help it. I am a weak woman, not a ſoldier.

I thought

I thought you had a duel with a person whom we have agreed never to mention. I thought you killed each other. I not only saw his sword, I *heard* it pass through my H.'s body. I saw you both die? and with you, love and gratitude. Who is there, thought I, to mourn for M.?——Not one!

You may call me foolish; but I am uneasy, miserable, wretched! indeed, indeed I am. For God's sake, let me hear from you.

LETTER XVI.

To the Same.

H. 24 Feb. 76.

THAT business, as I told you it would, last night, obliges him to go to town. I am to follow for the winter. Now, my H. for the royal black bob and the bit of chalk; or for any better scheme you'll plan. Let me know, to-morrow, where

you

you think Lady G.'s ſcheme will be moſt practicable on the road, and there I'll take care to ſtop. I take my bible oath I won't deceive you, and more welcome ſhall you be to my longing arms, than all the dukes or princes in chriſtendom. If I am not happy for one whole night in my life, it will now be your fault.

Is not this kind and thoughtful? Why did it ever occur to you, ſo often as we have talked of my being obliged to leave this dear place? To me *moſt* dear, ſince it has been the ſcene of my acquaintance, my happineſs with H.

But, am I to leave behind me that deareſt H.? Surely your recruiting buſineſs muſt be nearly over now. You *muſt* go to town. Though things can't often be contrived at the A, they may—they *may?*—they *ſhall* happen elſewhere.

Fail not to-morrow—and do not laugh at me any more about my dream. If it was a proof of my weakneſs, it was a proof alſo of my love.

I wiſh the day on which I am to ſet out from hence could be conjured about a month further back or ſo. Now, you aſk *why?* Look in your laſt year's almanack. Was not the *ſhorteſt day* ſome where about that time? Come, give me a kiſs for that, I am ſure I deſerve it.—Oh! fye Mr. H., not twenty. You are too generous in your payments. I muſt inſiſt upon returning you the overplus the next time we meet—that is to-morrow, you know.

LETTER XVII.

To Miſs ——.

Huntingdon, 26 Feb. 1776.

WHY will not the wiſhed-for day, or rather night, arrive? And here, I have not ſeen you ſince I know not when—not for two whole days.

But I wrote you a long letter yeſterday why it would be dangerous to meet; and all in rhyme. The beginning, I aſſure you,

you was not poetry, but truth——If the conclusion was coloured too highly, you must excuse it. The pencil of love executed it, and the sly rogue will indulge himself sometimes. Let the time come, I'll convince you his pencil did not much exaggerate.

Just now I was thinking of your birthday, about which I asked you the other day. It's droll that your's and mine should be so near together. And thus I observe thereon.

Your poets, cunning rogues, pretend
That men are made of clay;
And that the heavenly potters make
Some five or six a day.

No wonder, M. I and you
Don't quite detest each other;
Or that my soul is link'd to your's,
As if it were its brother:

For

For in one year we both were made,
  Nay almoſt in one day——
So, ten to one, we both came from
  One common heap of clay.

What? if I were not caſt in near
  So fine a mould as you—
My heart (or rather, M. *your's*)
  Is tender, fond, and true.

Corporal Trim ſets off to-day for our head quarters. My plan is laid ſo, that no diſcovery *can* take take place. Gods, that two ſuch ſouls, as your's and mine, ſhould be obliged to deſcend to arts and plans! Were it not for your dear ſake, I'd ſcorn to do any thing I would not wiſh diſcovered.

LETTER XVIII.

To Mr. ——.

H. 21 Feb. 1776.

ALL your plans are uſeleſs. The Corporal has made his forced march to no purpoſe. The fates are unkind. It is determined I am to go up *poſt*. So, we cannot poſſibly be happy together, as we hoped to have been had our own horſes drawn me up, in which caſe I muſt have ſlept upon the road. I am not clear old Robin Gray will not ſtay and attend me. Why cannot my Jamie? Cruel fortune! But in town we *will* be happy. When, again, ſhall I enjoy your dear ſociety; as I did during that, to me at leaſt, bleſſed ſnow? Nothing but my dear children could prevent our going with Cook to ſeek for happineſs in worlds unknown. There muſt be ſome corner of the globe where mutual affection is reſpected.

Don't

Don't forget to meet me. Scratch out *forget*: I know how much you think of me. Too much for your peace, nay for your health. Indeed my H. you don't look well. Pray be careful!

"Whatever wounds thy tender health,
"Will kill thy M.'s too."

Omiah is in good humour with me again. ——What kind of animal ſhould a naturaliſt expect from a native of Otaheite and an Huntingdonſhire dairy-maid? If my eyes don't deceive me, Mr. Omiah will give us a ſpecimen.—Will you bring me ſome book to-morrow to divert me, as I poſt it to town—that I may forget, if it be poſſible, I am poſting from you?

LETTER XIX.

To Miſs ——.

Hockerill, 1. March, 1776.

It is your ſtrict injunction that I do not offend you by ſuffering my pen to ſpeak of laſt night. I will not, my M. nor ſhould I, had you not injoined it. You once ſaid a nearer acquaintance would make me change my opinion of you. It has, I *have* changed my opinion. The more I know you, the more chaſtely I think of you. Notwithſtanding laſt night (what a night!), and our firſt too, I proteſt to God, I think of you with as much purity, as if we were going to be married——You take my meaning, I am ſure; becauſe they are the thoughts I know you wiſh me to entertain of you.

You got to town ſafe, I hope. *One* letter may find me before I ſhall be able to leave Huntingdon, whither I return to-day; or, at leaſt, to Cambridge. I am a fool about Crop, you know. And I am now more

more tender of him, becauſe he has carried *you*.—How little did we think that morning we ſhould ever make each other ſo happy!

Don't forget to write, and don't forget the key, againſt I come to town. As far as ſeeing you, I will uſe it ſometimes; but never for an opportunity to indulge our paſſion. That, poſitively, ſhall never again happen under *his* roof. How did we applaud each other for not ſuffering his walls at H. to be inſulted with the firſt ſcene of it! And how happy were we both, after we waked from our dream of bliſs, to think how often we had acted otherwiſe, during the time the ſnow ſhut me up at H.! a ſnow as dear to me, as to yourſelf.

My mind is torn, rent, with ten thouſand thoughts and reſolutions about you, and about myſelf.

When we meet, which ſhall be as we fixed, I may perhaps mention *one* idea to you.

Pray let us contrive to be together ſome evening that your favourite Jephtha is performed.

Inclosed is a song, which came into my hands by an accident since we parted. Neither the words nor the music, I take it, will displease you.

Adieu.

SONG.

When your beauty appears
In its graces and airs,
All bright as an angel new dropp'd from the sky;
At distance I gaze, and am awed by my fears,
So strangely you dazzle my eye!

But when, without art,
Your kind thoughts you impart,
When love runs in blushes thro' every vein;
When it darts from your eyes, when it pants in your heart,
Then I know your'e a woman again.

" There's a passion and pride
" In your sex," she replied,
" And thus might I gratify both, I would do;
" As an angel appear to each lover beside,
" But still be a woman to you."

LETTER XX.

To the Same.

Cannon Coffee-houſe, Charing-Croſs,
17 March, 76.

No further than this can I get from you, before I aſſure you that every word I ſaid juſt now came from the bottom of my heart. I never ſhall be happy, never ſhall be in my ſenſes, till you conſent to marry me. And notwithſtanding the dear night at Hockerill, and the other which your ingenuity procured me laſt week in D. ſtreet, I ſwear by the bliſs of bliſſes, I never will taſte it again till you are my wife.

LETTER XXI.

To the Same.

Cannon Coffee-houſe,
17 March, 76.

THOUGH you can hardly have read my laſt ſcrawl, I muſt peſter you with another.

I had

has been *your* part, from the beginning of the piece, to *mine?* I was obliged to act a part even to *you*. It was my buſineſs not to let you ſee how unhappy the artifices, to which I have ſubmitted, made me. And that they did embitter even our happieſt moments.

But fate ſtands between us. We are doomed to be wretched. And I, every now and then, think ſome terrible cataſtrophe will come of our connection. "Some dire event," as Storge prophetically ſays in Jephtha, "hangs o'er our heads;——

"Some woeful ſong we have to ſing
"In miſery extreme.—O never, never
"Was my foreboding mind diſtreſs'd before
"With ſuch inceſſant pangs!"

Oh, that it were no crime to quit this world like Faldoni and Tereſa! and that we might be happy together in ſome other world, where gold and ſilver are unknown!

By

By your hand I could even die with pleasure. I know I could.

"Insuperable reason." Yes, my H., there is, and you force it from me. Yet, better to tell you, than to have you doubt my love; that love which is now my religion. I have hardly any God but you. I almost offer up my prayers *to* you, as well as *for* you.

Know then, if you was to marry me, you would marry some hundred pounds worth of debts! and *that* you never shall do.

Do you remember a solemn oath you took in one of your letters, when I was down at H.? and how you told me afterwards it *must* be so, because you had so solemnly sworn it?

In the same solemn and dreadful words I swear that I never will marry you, happy as it would make me, while I owe a shilling in the world. Jephtha's vow is past.

What your letter says about my poor children made me weep; but it shall not make me change my resolution.

It

It is a further reaſon why I ſhould not.—"If I do not marry you, I do not love you!" Gracious powers of love! Does my H. ſay ſo? my *not* marrying you is the ſtrongeſt proof I can give you of my love. And Heaven, you know, has heard my vow. Do *you* reſpect it, and never tempt me to break it—for not even *you* will *ever* ſucceed.—Till I have ſome better portion than debts, I *never* will be your's.

Then what is to be done? you aſk. Why, I'll tell you, H. Your determination to drop all particular intercourſe till marriage has made us one, flatters me more than I can tell you, becauſe it ſhews me your opinion of me in the ſtrongeſt light; it almoſt reſtores me to my own good opinion. The copy of verſes you brought me on that ſubject, is ſuperior to any thing I ever read. They ſhall be thy M.'s morning prayer, and her evening ſong. While you are in Ireland——

Yes, my love, in Ireland. Be ruled by me.

me. You ſhall immediately join your regiment there. You know it is your duty. In the mean time, ſomething may happen. Heaven will not deſert two faithful hearts that love like your's and mine. There are joys; there is happineſs in ſtore for us yet. I feel there is. And (as I ſaid juſt now) *while you are in Ireland*, I'll write to you *every* poſt, *twice* by *one* poſt, and I'll think of you, and I'll dream of you, and I'll kiſs your picture, and I'll wipe my eyes, and I'll kiſs it again, and then I'll weep again. And——

Can I give a ſtronger inſtance of my regard for you, or a ſtronger proof that you ought to take my advice, than my thus begging my only joy to leave me? I will not ſwear I ſhall ſurvive it; but, I beſeech you, go!

Fool that I am—I undo with one hand, all I do with the other. My tears, which drop between every word I write, prevent the effect of my reaſoning; which, I am ſure, is juſt.

Be

Be a man, I ſay—you *are* an angel. Join your regiment; and, as ſure as I love you (nothing can be *more* ſure) I will recall you, from what will be baniſhment as much to me as to you, the firſt moment I can marry you with honour to myſelf, and happineſs to you.

But, I muſt not write thus.

Adieu!

Ill ſuits the voice of love, when glory calls,
And bids thee follow Jephtha to the field.

LETTER XXIII.

To Miſs——.

Cannon Coffe-houſe,
17 March, 1776.

And I will reſpect the vow of Jephtha, and I will follow to the field. At leaſt, I will think of it all to-night, for I am ſure I ſhall not ſleep, and will let you know the ſucceſs of my ſtruggle, for a ſtruggle it will be to-morrow. I will wait for you at the ſame place

place in the park, where I ſhall ſee you open the A. door. Should it rain—I'll write. It was my intention to have endeavoured to ſee you now, but I changed my mind, and wrote this, here; and I am glad I did. We are not in a condition to ſee each other. Cruel debts! Rather, cruel vow! for, would you but have let me, I would have contrived ſome ſcheme about your debts. I *could* form a plan. My Goſport matters —my commiſſion——

Alas, you frown, and I muſt ſtop. Why would not fortune ſmile upon my two lottery tickets? Heaven knows I bought them on your account. Upon the back of one of them I wrote, in caſe of my ſudden death, "this is the property of Miſs—." On the back of the other, that it belonged to your daughter.

For what am I ſtill reſerved?

L E T-

LETTER XXIV.

To Mr———.

A. 19 March, 1776.

Why, why do you write to me ſo often? Why do you ſee me ſo often? When you acknowledge the neceſſity of complying with my advice.

You tell me, if I bid you, you'll go. I have bid you, begged you to go.—I *do* bid you go. Go, I conjure you, go! But let us not have any more partings. The laſt was too, too much. I did not recover myſelf all day. And your goodneſs to my little white-headed boy—He made me burſt into tears this morning, by talking of the good-natured gentleman, and producing your preſent.

Either ſtay, and let our affection diſcover and ruin us—or go.

On the bended knees of love I entreat you, H., my deareſt H. to go.

LETTER XXV.

To Miss ——.

Ireland, 26 March, 1776.

IRELAND—England—Good Heavens, that M. should be in one part of the world, and her H. in another! Will not our destinies suffer us to breathe the same air? Mine will not, I most firmly believe, let me rest, till they have hunted me to death.

Will you not give me your approbation for obeying you thus? Approbation! And is that the coin to pass between *us?*

Yet, I will obey you further. I will restrain my pen as much as possible. I will scratch the word love out of my dictionary. I will forget—I lie—I never *can*, nor ever *will* forget you, or any thing which belongs to you. But I will, as you wisely advise, and kindly desire me, as much as possible, write on other subjects. Every thing entertaining, that I can procure, I will. I'll *Twissify*, and write Tours—or any thing

but

but love-letters. This morning, pardon me: I am unable to trifle; I *muſt* be allowed to talk of love, of M.

And, when I *am* able, you muſt allow me to put in a word or two ſometimes for myſelf. To-day, however, I will not make *you* unhappy by telling you how truly ſo *I* am.

The truth is—my heart is full; and though I thought, when I took up my pen, I could have filled a quire of paper with it, I now have not a word to ſay. Were I ſitting by your ſide now (oh that I were!) I ſhould only have power to recline my cheek upon your ſhoulder, and to wet your hankerchief with my tears.

My own ſafety, but for your ſake, is the laſt of my conſiderations. Our paſſage was rather boiſterous, but not dangerous. Mrs. F. (whom I mentioned to you, I believe, in the letter I wrote juſt before we embarked) has enabled me to make you laugh with an account of her behaviour; were either of us in a humour to laugh.

Why

Why did you cheat me ſo about that box?

Had I known I ſhould find, upon open-it, that the things were for me, I would never have brought it. But that you knew. Was it kind, my M. to give me ſo many *daily* mĕmorandums of you, when I was to be at ſuch a diſtance from you? Oh, yes, it was, it was, *moſt* kind. And that, and you, and all your thouſand and ten thouſand kindneſſes I never will forget. The purſe ſhall be my conſtant companion, the ſhirts I'll wear by night, one of the handkerchiefs I was obliged to uſe in drying my eyes as ſoon as I opened the box, the——

God, God, bleſs you in this world—that is, give you your H.—, and grant you an eaſy paſſage to eternal bleſſings in a better world.

H.!

LETTER XXVI.

To the Same.

Ireland, 8 April, 1776.

YOUR'S, dated April the firſt, would have diverted me, had I been ſome leagues nearer to you. It contained true wit and humour. I truly thank you for it, becauſe I know with how much difficulty you ſtudy for any thing like wit or humour in the preſent ſituation of your mind. But you do it to divert me; and it is done for one, who, though he cannot laugh at it, as he ought, will remember it, as he ought—Yet, with what a melancholy tenderneſs it concluded! *There* ſpoke your heart.

Your ſituation, when you wrote it, was ſomething like that of an actreſs, who ſhould be obliged to play a part in comedy, on the evening of a day which, by ſome real cataſtrophe, had marked her out for the capital figure of a real tragedy. Perhaps I have ſaid ſomething like this in the long letter

letter I have written you ſince. Never mind.

Pray be careful how you ſeal your letters. The wax always robs me of five or ſix words. Leave a ſpace for your ſeal. Suppoſe that ſhould be the part of your letter which tells me you ſtill love me. If the wax cover it, I ſee it not—I find no ſuch expreſſion in your letter,—I grow diſtracted—and immediately ſet out for Charing-Croſs to aſk you whether you do indeed ſtill love me.

In the hoſpitality of this country I was not deceived. They have a curſe in their language, ſtrongly deſcriptive of it—"May the graſs grow at your door!"—The women, if I knew not you, I ſhould find ſenſible and pretty. But I am deaf, dumb, blind, to every thing, and to every perſon but you. If I write any more this morning, I ſhall certainly ſin againſt your commands.

Why do you ſay nothing of your dear children? I inſiſt upon it you buy my

friend

friend a taw, and two dozen of marbles; and place them to the account of

Your humble Servant.

LETTER XXVII.

To the Same.

Ireland, 20 April, 76.

THANKS for the two letters I received laſt week. They drew tears from me, but not tears of ſorrow.

To my poetry you are much too partial. Never talk of writing poetry for the preſs. It will not do. Few are they, who like you, can judge of poetry; and, of the judges, few, alas! are juſt. Juvenal, the Roman Churchill, adviſes a young man to turn auctioneer, rather than poet. In our days, Chriſtie would knock Chatterton out of all chance in a week.—The Spaniards have a proverb, "He, who cannot make one verſe, is a block-head; he who makes more, is a fool."—Pythagoras you know a little by name. Perhaps you

you may not know he was ſtarved to death in the temple of the Muſes at Metapontum. The Muſes have no temples, it is true, in our days (for God knows they are not much worſhipped now) but the Ladies are not without their human ſacrifices.

A young man was complaining the other day that he had loſt his appetite; "Turn Poet, then," ſaid one in company, "they generally have pretty ſtout ones."

Your *ſenſible* eyes have not long, I know, been dry from the tale of Chatterton. Even now, a pearly drop peeps over the brim of each; and now they drop, drop upon his mangled memory, like the Samaritan's balm upon the traveller's wounds.——And, perhaps, what I had heard and told you may not be half.

That I may make you ſome amends for teizing you with my bad poetry the other day, I will to-day ſend you ſome very good. It is the compoſition of a clergyman, an Engliſhman, ſettled near Dublin. It got the prize at Oxford not long ſince, and was ſpoken in the theatre at ſuch a public buſineſs, as one at which, I think, I remember to have heard you ſay you were preſent. Perhaps you were there this very time.

When you have read the lines, you will think I need not add a word about the author's abilities.

On the Love of our Country.

YE ſouls illuſtrious, who, in days of yore,
With peerleſs might the Britiſh target bore,
Who, clad in wolf-ſkin, from the ſcythed car,
Frown'd on the iron brow of mailed war;
Who dar'd your rudely painted limbs oppoſe
To ſteel of Chalybs, and to Roman foes:
And ye of later age, tho' not leſs fame
In tilt and tournament, the princely game
Of Arthur's barons, won't, in hardieſt ſport,
To claim the faireſt Guerdon of the Court;
Say, holy ſhades, did e'er your gen'rous blood
Roll thro' your faithful ſons in nobler flood,
Than * late, when George bade gird on ev'ry thigh
The myrtle-braided ſword of liberty;

* Theſe lines were written ſoon after the inſtallation at Windſor, by the Rev. Christopher Butson, chaplain to the Right Honourable the Lord Chancellor.

Th

Say, when the high-born Druids' magic ſtrain
Rouz'd on old Mona's top a female train
To madneſs, and with more than mortal rage
Bade them like furies in the fight engage,
Frantic when each unbound her briſtling hair,
And ſhook a flaming torch, and yell'd in wild deſpair;
Or when on Creſſy's plain the ſable might
Of Edward dar'd four monarchs to the fight;
Say, holy ſhades, did patriotic heat
In your big hearts, with quicker tranſports beat
Than in your ſons, when forth like ſtorms they pour'd,
In freedom's cauſe, the fury of the ſword?
Who rul'd the main, or gallant armies led,
With *Hawke* who conquer'd, or with *Wolf* who bled.

Poor is his triumph, and diſgrac'd his name,
Who draws the ſword for empire, wealth, or fame;
For him tho' wealth be blown on ev'ry wind,
Tho' fame announce him mightieſt of mankind,
Tho' twice ten nations ſink beneath his blade,
Virtue diſowns him, and his glories fade.
For him no pray'rs are pour'd, no pæans ſung,
No bleſſings chaunted from a nations tongue,
Blood marks the path to his untimely bier,
The curſe of widows and the orphan's tear

E Cry

Cry to high Heaven for vengeance on his head;
Alive, deserted; and accurst, when dead.
Indignant of his deeds, the muse, who sings
Undaunted truth, and scorns to flatter kings,
Shall shew the monster in his hideous form,
And mark him as an earthquake, or a storm.

Not so the patriot chief, who dar'd withstand
The base invader of his native land;
Who made her weal his noblest, only end,
Rul'd but to serve her, fought but to defend,
Her voice in council, and in fight her sword,
Lov'd as her father, as her god ador'd;
Who firmly virtuous, and severely brave,
Sunk with the freedom that he could not save.
On worth like his, the muse delights to wait,
Reveres alike in triumph or defeat,
Crowns with true glory and with spotless fame,
And honours *Paoli's* more than *Frederick's* name.

Here let the muse withdraw the blood-stain'd veil,
And shew the boldest son of public zeal.
See Sidney leaning o'er the block! His mein,
His voice, his hand, unshaken, clear, serene.
Yet no harangue, proudly declaimed aloud,
To gain the plaudit of a wayward crowd;
No specious vaunt death's terrors to defy,
Still death delaying, as afraid to die.

But

But ſternly ſilent, down he bows—to prove
How firm his virtuous, though miſtaken love.
Unconquer'd patriot! form'd by ancient lore
The love of ancient freedom to reſtore,
Who nobly acted, what he boldly wrote.
And ſeal'd by death the leſſons that he taught.

Dear is the tie that links the anxious ſire,
To the fond babe that prattles round his fire;
Dear is the love that prompts the grateful youth
His ſire's fond cares and drooping age to ſooth;
Dear is the brother, ſiſter, huſband, wife;
Dear all the charities of ſocial life:
Nor wants firm friendſhip holy wreaths to bind,
In mutual ſympathy the faithful mind:
But not th' endearing ſprings that fondly move
To filial duty, or parental love,
Not all the ties that kindred boſoms bind,
Not all in friendſhip's holy wreaths entwin'd,
Are half ſo dear, ſo potent to controul
The gen'rous workings of the patriot ſoul,
As is that holy voice which cancels all
Thoſe ties, which bids him for his country fall;
At this high ſummons, with undaunted zeal,
He bares his breaſt, invites th' impending ſteel,
Smiles at the hand that deals the fatal blow,
Nor heaves one ſigh for all he leaves below.

Nor yet doth glory, tho' her port be bold
Her aſpect radiant, and her treſſes gold,
Guide thro' the walks of death alone her car,
Attendant only on the din of war:
She not diſdains the gentler vale of peace,
Nor olive ſhades of philoſophic eaſe,
Where heav'n taught minds to wooe the muſe reſort,
Create in colours, or with ſounds tranſport;
Where youths court ſcience, or where ſages teach,
Where ſtateſmen plan, where mitred fathers preach——
More pleas'd on Iſis' ſilent marge to roam,
Than bear in pomp the ſpoils of Minden home.

To read with Newton's ken the ſtarry ſky,
And God the ſame in all his orbs deſcry;
To lead forth merit from her humble ſhade;
Extend to riſing arts a patron's aid;
Build the nice ſtructure of the gen'rous law,
That holds the free-born ſoul in willing awe;
O'er pale misfortune drop, with friendly ſigh,
Pity's mild balm, and wipe affliction's eye;
Theſe, theſe are deeds Britannia muſt approve,
Muſt nurſe their growth with all a parent's love.
Theſe are the deeds that public virtue owns.
And, juſt to public virtue, glory crowns.

LETTER XXVIII.

To the Same.

Ireland, 3d May, 1776.

My laſt, I hope, did not offend you. The bank note I was obliged to return; although I thank you for it more than words can tell you.

Shall I, whom you will not marry, becauſe you will not load me with your debts, increaſe thoſe debts; at leaſt prevent you from diminiſhing them, by robbing you of fifty pounds? Were I capable of it, I ſhould be unworthy your love. But be not offended that I returned it. Heaven knows how willingly a quire of ſuch things ſhould have accompanied it, had Heaven made me ſo rich.

Be not anxious about me. Talk not of the poſtage which your dear letters coſt me. Will you refuſe to make your H. happy? And think you I can pay too dear for happineſs?

But, Lord! you rave. I am rich—as rich as a Jew: and without taking into the calculation the treaſure I poſſeſs in your love.——Why, you talk of what I allow that relation, poor ſoul! that does not ſwallow up all my lands and hereditaments at Goſport. Then there's my pay, and twenty other ways and means beſides, I dare ſay, could I but recollect them.—Go to—I tell you I *am* rich. So, let me know you got the ſilver paper ſafe, and that I am a good boy.

Rich! To be ſure I am—why, I can afford to go to plays. I ſaw Catley laſt night, in your favourite character.—By the way, I'll tell you a ſtory of her, when ſhe was on your ſide the water.

Names do not immortalize praiſe-worthy anecdotes, they immortalize names.—Some difference had ariſen between Miſs Catley and the managers concerning the terms upon which ſhe was to be engaged for the ſeaſon. One of the managers called upon her, at her little lodgings in Drury-lane, to to ſettle it. The maid was going to ſhew the gentleman up ſtairs, and to call her miſtreſs. " No, no," cries the actreſs who was in the kitchen, and heard the manager's voice, " there is no occaſion to ſhew " the gentleman to a room.—I am buſy " below, (to the manager) making apple " dumplings for my brats. You know " whether you have a mind to give me the " money I aſk, or not. I am none of " your fine ladies, who get a cold or the " tooth-ach, and can't ſing. If you have " a mind to give me the money, ſay ſo; " my mouth ſhall not open for a farthing " leſs. So, good morning to you—and " don't keep the girl there in the paſſage; " for I want her to put the dumplings in " the pot, while I nurſe the child.—The turnips of Fabricius, and Andrew Marvel's cold leg of mutton, are worthy to be ſerved up on the ſame day with Nan Catley's apple-dumplings.

Come—I am not unhappy, or I could not talk of other people and write thus gaily. Nothing can make me truly unhappy, but a change in your ſentiments of me. By the Almighty God of heaven, I know my own feelings ſo thoroughly, I do not think I could ſurvive ſuch a thing.

As you love me, ſcold me not about the poplin you'll receive next week. It coſt me nothing—I may ſurely give what was given to me.

LETTER XXIX.

To the Same.

Ireland,
29th May, 1776.

Do you think, that to make ſuch propoſals, as your laſt contained, is the way to reconcile me to this worſe than baniſhment? You refuſed to come into my ſcheme of marriage--Nothing ſhall tempt me to come into your ſcheme. Perſiſt in your idea of going on the ſtage; and, as I live, I'll come over and make a party to damn you the firſt night of your appearance. Since you

you will not ſhare my fortunes, I will not ſhare your earnings.

The ſtory you mention at Flamborough, of Boardingham, who was murdered by his wife and her lover, is moſt ſhocking. The reflections you draw from it are moſt juſt; and what you ſay of our ſituation moſt true. The woman muſt have been beyond a wild beaſt ſavage. Yet their feelings, when ſhe and Aikney were at the gallows together (ſuppoſing any thing like love remained) muſt have been exquiſite.— I proteſt, I would willingly embrace with M. the cruelleſt death which torture could invent (provided ſhe were on a bed of roſes), than lead the happieſt life without her. ——What viſions have I conjured up!— my pen drops from my hand.——

Your catch upon a bumper I like much. It beats, both in words and muſic, "a bumper 'Squire Jones." By the way what an old word it is! Let me make a linguiſt of you to-day.

The learned Johnſon deriveth *bumper* ("a cup filled till the liquor ſwells over the "brims") from *bump*, which cometh, he ſaith, from *bum*, perhaps, as being prominent; the which *bum* cometh, we are told, from *bomme*, (Dutch) and ſignifieth "the part on which we ſit."——The word *bumper* is by ſome writer derived from *bon-pere*, the uſual familiar phraſe for prieſts, who were ſuppoſed not to diſlike *bumpers*.—This I may ſay—if "a cup filled till the "liquor ſwells over the brims" comes from "the part on which we ſit," it muſt be granted, as a French poet ſays of *Alfana's* coming from *equus*.

Qu'en venant de la, juſqu' icy,
Il a bien changé ſur la route.

And now I have ended in good ſpirits, as well as you. I remember the time when Hamlet might have ſaid to me, as he does to Horatio,

"Thou

"Thou haſt no revenue but thy good ſpirits
"To feed and cloath thee."

Now, I have got a little revenue, which M. will not ſhare with me, and God knows who has got my good ſpirits—Well, I muſt not think.

LETTER XXX.

To the Same.

Ireland, 18 June, 76.

My Laura is not angry with me, I hope, for the three or four *tender* letters I have written to her ſince the beginning of this month. And yet, your's of yeſterday ſeems to ſay you are. If I bear my ſituation like a man, will you not allow me to feel it like a man?

Misfortune, like a creditor ſevere,
But riſes in demand for her delay.
She makes a ſcourge of paſt proſperity,
To ſting me more, and double my diſtreſs.

But

This country's facetious Dean ſaid, his friend Arbuthnot could do every thing but walk. My friend can do every thing but loſe at cards.

Feeling, and all the commanding powers of the mind, were never perhaps before ſo mixed up together. A tale of ſorrow will make his little eyes wink, wink, wink, like a green girls. Before the company came laſt night, I ſhewed him "Auld Robin Gray"; and, though he had ſeen it before, he could not get over "My mother could na ſpeak," without winking. For the credit of your ſide of the water, he is an Engliſhman. His agreeable wife, by her beauty and accompliſhments, does credit to this country. She is remarkable alſo for her feeling, though in a different way. You ſhall relate an anecdote of diſtreſs, or read a ſtory of ill uſage, and, while his eyes are winking for the object of the ill uſage or the diſtreſs, her's ſhall be ſtriking fire with rage againſt the author of it. "Good God! ſhe exclaims, "if that villain

villain was but in my power!—" And I ſometimes think ſhe is going to ring for her hat and cloak, that ſhe may ſally forth, and pull his houſe about his ears.—Bound up together (as they are, and as I hope they will long continue) they form a complete ſyſtem of humanity.——

It would have gratified me much to have been with you when Garrick took his farewel of the ſtage. Do you remember the laſt paper in the *Idler* upon its being the *laſt*? The reflection that it was the *laſt* time Garrick would ever play, was, in itſelf, painful. How, my Laura, my M. my life, ſhall I bear it, if I ever ſhould be doomed to take my laſt leave, my laſt look of you!——

—In what I wrote this morning I mentioned the *Idler*. A curious letter was ſhewn me the other day by a clergyman, which he aſſures me is authentic, and was written by the late Lord Gower to a friend of Dean Swift. As I know how you admire the

eminent

eminent person whom it concerns, I send it to you.

"Mr. Samuel Johnson (author of *London*, a satire, and some other poetical pieces) is a native of this country, and much respected by some worthy gentlemen in his neighbourhood, who are trustees of a charity-school now vacant, the certain salary of which is sixty pounds per annum, of which they are desirous to make him master; but unfortunately he is not capable of receiving their bounty, which would make him happy for life, by not being Master of Arts, which by the statutes of this school the master of it must be. Now these gentlemen do me the honour to think that I have interest enough in you to prevail upon you to write to dean Swift to persuade the University of Dublin to send a diploma to me, constituting this poor man Master of Arts in their University. They highly extol the man's learning and probity, and will not be persuaded that the University will make any difficulty of conferring such a favour upon a stranger, if he is recommended by the Dean.——They say he is not afraid of the strictest examination, though he is off so long a journey; but will venture if the Dean thinks it necessary, choosing rather to die upon the road, than to be starved to death in translating for boksellers, which has been his only subsistence for some time past. I fear there is more difficulty in this affair than these good-natured gen-

tlemen

tlemen apprehend; especially as their election cannot be delayed longer than the 10th of next month. If you see this matter in the same light it appears to me, I hope you will burn this, and pardon me for giving you so much trouble about an impracticable thing: but if you think there is a probability of obtaining the favour asked, I am sure your humanity and propensity to relieve merit in distress, will incline you to serve the poor man, without my adding any more to the trouble I have already given you, than assuring you I am, with great truth, &c.

Trentham, Aug. 1, 1737.

One other subject for your reflection, and I have done.

What must have been Johnson's feelings, when, in his wonderful work, the English Dictionary, he cited the following passage from Ascham, as an instance of the use of the word *Men*? "Wits live obscurely, men care not how; or die obscurely, men mark not when."

LETTER

in the ſame country with you)—He will call at the Cannon coffee-houſe for me. Do ſend me, thither, the French book you mention, *Werther*. If you don't, I poſitively never will forgive you. Nonſenſe, to ſay it will make me unhappy, or that I ſhan't be able to read it! Muſt I piſtol myſelf, becauſe a thick-blooded German has been fool enough to ſet the example; or becauſe a German noveliſt has feigned ſuch a ſtory? If *you* don't lend it me, I will moſt aſſuredly procure it ſome time or another; ſo, you may as well have the merit of obliging me.—My friend will ſend a ſmall parcel for you to D. ſtreet. The books I ſend you, becauſe I know you have not got them, and becauſe they are ſo much cheaper here. If you are afraid of emptying my purſe (which by the way is almoſt worn out), you ſhall be my debtor for them. So, ſend me a note of hand, *value receiv'd.* The other things are ſurely not worth mentioning.

LETTER XXXIII.

To Mr. ——.

England, 20 Aug. 76.

For God's ſake! where are you? What is the matter? Why don't you write?— Are you ill? God forbid! And I not with you to nurſe you! if you are, why don't you let ſomebody elſe write to you? Better all ſhould be diſcovered, than ſuffer what I ſuffer. It's more than a month ſince I heard from you. A month uſed to bring me eight or ten letters. When I grew uneaſy, it was in vain, as I ſaid in my laſt, that I endeavoured to find your friend who brought the parcel (for I would certainly have ſeen him, and aſked him about you). What is become of all my letters for this laſt month? Did you get what I returned by your friend? Do you like the purſe? The book you mentioned, is juſt the only book you ſhould never read. On my knees, I beg you never, never read it! Perhaps you

you have read it—Perhaps!—I am diſtracted——Heaven only knows to whom I may be writing this letter.

Madam, or Sir!

If you are a woman, I think you will; if you are a man, and ever loved, I am ſure you will, oblige me with one line to ſay what is come of Mr.—— of the —— regiment. Direct to Mrs. ——, D. ſtreet, London.—Any perſon whoſe hand my letter may fall into, will not think this much trouble; and, if they ſend me good news, Heaven knows how a woman, who loves, if poſſible, too well, will thank them.

LETTER XXXIV.

To Miſs ——.

Ireland, 10 Sept. 1776.

As I am no ſportſman, there is no merit, you may think, in devoting a morning to this employment. Nor do I claim any merit. 'Tis only making myſelf happy.

Now, I hope, you are quite at eaſe about

me.

me. My health, upon my honour! upon our love! is almoſt re-eſtabliſhed—Were I not determined to keep on *this* ſide the truth, I would ſay *quite*. The four letters I have written to you, ſince I received your frantic ſheet of paper, have explained and made up every thing. How can I ſufficiently thank you for all your letters? Eſpecially for that of this week? Never did you pen a better. Did I know any body employed in a work, where that letter could properly appear, he ſhould inſert it in your own words.

Excuſe me, I am unwillingly called away.

What I ſaid this morning about your letter, brings to my recollection ſomething of that ſort. Shall I tell it you? I will.

James Hirſt, in the year 1711, lived ſervant with the honourable Edward Wortley. It happened, one day, in re-delivering a parcel of letters to his maſter, by miſtake he gave him one which he had written to his ſweetheart, and kept back one of Mr. Wortley's. He ſoon diſcovered the miſtake, and hurried back to his maſ-

te

ter; but unfortunately for poor James, it happened to be the firſt that preſented itſelf to Mr. Wortley, and, before James returned, he had given way to a curioſity which led him to open it, and read the love-told ſtory of an enamoured footman. It was in vain that James begged to have it returned. "No," ſays Mr. Wortley, "James, you ſhall be a great man, this letter ſhall appear in the Spectator."

Mr. Wortley communicated the letter to his friend Sir Richard Steel.—It was accordingly publiſhed in his own words, and is that letter, No. 71, volume the firſt of the Spectator, beginning "Dear Betty."

James found means to remove that unkindneſs of which he complains in his leter; but, alas! before their wiſhes were compleated, a ſpeedy end was put to a paſſion which would not diſcredit much ſuperior rank, by the unexpected death of Betty. James, out of the great regard and love he bore to Betty, after her death, married the ſiſter. He died, not many

years

years ſince, in the neighbourhood of Wortley, near Leeds, Yorkſhire.

To marry you is the utmoſt of my wiſhes; but, remember, I don't engage to marry your ſiſter in caſe of your death.—Death! How can I think of ſuch a thing, though it be but in joke.

LETTER XXXV.

To the Same.

Ireland, 15 Sept. 1776.

THE commands of your laſt letter, for the reaſons you give, I have immediately obeyed.—My * enquiries about the young Engliſhman you mention, amount to this. He is is liked tolerably well here. He would be liked more, if he took more pains to be liked. His contempt for ſome people in the world, whom others deſpiſe perhaps as well as he, is ſometimes too conſpicuous. Accident, has given me an opportunity to ſee and know a great deal of

* His own character.

him; and with certainty. His heart is certainly not bad. His abilities are as certainly not equal to what he once confeſſes to have thought them; perhaps they are ſuperior to the opinion he now entertains of them. He has ambition and emulation enough to have almoſt ſupplied any want of genius, and to have made him almoſt any thing, had he fallen into proper hands. But his ſchool-maſters knew nothing of the human heart, nor over much of the head. Though indolent to a degree, a keen eye might have diſcovered, may ſtill diſcover, induſtry at the bottom; a good cultivator might have turned it, may ſtill turn it, to good account. His friendſhips are warm, ſincere, decided——his enmities the ſame. He complains, now and then, that ſome of his friends will pretend to know him better than they know themſelves, and better than they know any thing elſe. "They would play upon him; they would "ſeem to know his ſtops; they pretend to "be able to ſound him from his loweſt note,

"to

"to the top of his compaſs; and there is "much muſic, excellent voice, in a little "pipe, yet cannot they make it ſpeak. "Do they think," he demands, "that he "is eaſier to be play'd than a pipe?"—— Why, really, I do not think this is the caſe at preſent, whatever it may have been. Secreſy is not brought *into* the world, it is acquired in the world. An honeſt heart can only acquire it by experience. The character which he had certainly gotten ſome how among ſome of his intimates, has been of ſervice both to them and to himſelf. They made a point of ſecrecy, after they choſe to diſcover a want of it in him; and now he has made a point of it himſelf. My deareſt ſecret (*you* know what that is) ſhould now ſooner be truſted to him than to any of his former accuſers. The loudeſt of them, to my knowledge, was little calculated to judge; for though he might not abſolutely think him a coward, he certainly did not ſuſpect his friend of courage, till ſufficient proof of it was given under his own eye. Now, in my opinion, true courage and reſolution are this gentleman's marking characteriſtics. This is no great compliment; for, without them, I would not give a farthing for any man.

Such, in my judgment, is the young gentleman about whom you wiſhed me to enquire, and with whom I happen to have lived a good deal. His principal merit is, that my amiable friend (the mention of whoſe wife juſt jogged your jealouſy) ſincerely loves him. That worthy man ſeldom throws away his attachment where it is not deſerved. Nor do I know any thing in the gentleman, whoſe character I have been ſketching, which gives me more pleaſure, or which it would give him more pleaſure to have noticed, than the love and reſpect which I am ſure he feels for my friend; unleſs perhaps his affectionate ſenſe of the obligations which I believe I have told you he lies under to a Mr. B.——

So much for buſineſs. Now for an article of news. The latter end of laſt

month,

month, a lady and her fervant, as they were riding in Phoenix Park, were ftopped by a man on foot; very genteelly dreffed in white cloaths, and a gold laced hat. He demanded the lady's money, which fhe gave him, amounting to 26 guineas. The perfon put the cafh into one of his pockets, and took from the other a fmall diamond hoop ring, which he prefented to the lady, defiring her to wear it for the fake of an extraordinary robber, who made it a point of honour to take no more from a beautiful lady, than he could make a return for in value. He then, with great agility, vaulted over the wall, and difappeared.

This you may perhaps call an Irifh way of robbing. There certainly was fomething original in it. The gentleman feems clearly to imagine, that an exchange is no robbery.——

As to your threat, I will anfwer it in the fame ftyle—"I *will* love you—and if—!" But neither my anfwer, nor your threat, is original. Reading, this morning,

 a hiftory

a hiſtory of this country, I found the following anecdote, in 1487, a dreadful war was carried on in Ulſter, between the Chieftain O'Neal, and the neighbouring Chieftain of Tirconnel. This war had nothing more conſiderable for its immediate cauſe, than the pride of O'Neal, who demanded that his enemy ſhould recognize his authority by paying tribute. The laconic ſtyle, in which the demand was made and rejected, would not have diſgrac'd a nobler conteſt. "Send me tribute—or elſe!"—was the meſſage of O'Neal. To which was returned, with the ſame princely brevity,—"I owe you none "and if—!"—But I talk nonſenſe. This does not prove your threat to have been borrowed; for I dare ſay, you never heard of O'Neal till this moment. It only proves that two people may expreſs themſelves alike.

Should any man who loved like me (if any man ever did love like me) have ſpoken of his love in terms like thoſe I uſe to ſpeak of mine, follows it therefore that I

have

have borrowed either his paſſion or his language? Were it poſſible for you to think ſo, I never would forgive you.—Pray copy the muſic you mention in your next.

LETTER XXXVI.

To the Same.

Ireland, 18 Sep. 76.

How happens it that I have not ſooner noticed what you ſay, in a letter the beginning of laſt month, about the new puniſhment of working upon the Thames? Politicians may write more learned upon the matter but I will defy Beccaria to write more feelingly or humanely. There certainly is much truth in what you ſay. Experience however will be the beſt teſt. Perhaps my true reaſon for noticing your ſenſible letter thus late, was to introduce a ſcene which paſſed in the quickſilver mines of Idra, a ſtill more unpleaſant abode than Mr. Campbell's academy. This uſed to be

Colonel G.'s method, you remember, of introducing his home-made jokes. Not that my ſtory is home-made—I take it from ſome Italian letters a brother officer lent me, written by Mr. Everard, and I give it you almoſt in his own words—except in one or two paſſages, where I think he has loſt an opportunity of ſurprizing the reader.

"The pleaſure I always take in writing to you, wherever I am, and whatever doing, in ſome meaſure diſpels my preſent uneaſineſs; an uneaſineſs cauſed at once by the diſagreeable aſpect of every thing around me, and the more diſagreeable ſcene to which I have been witneſs.

Something too I have to tell you of Count Alberti. You remember him one of the gayeſt, moſt agreeable perſons at the Court of Vienna; at once the example of the men, and the favourite of the fair ſex. I often heard you repeat his name with eſteem, as one of the few that did honour to the preſent age; as poſſeſſed of generoſity and pity in the higheſt degree; as one who made no other uſe of fortune, but to alleviate the diſtreſſes of mankind. But firſt of all, the ſcene I mentioned.

After paſſing ſeveral parts of the Alps, and having viſited Germany, I thought I could not well re-

turn

turn home, without viſiting the quickſilver mines at Idra, and ſeeing thoſe dreadful ſubterranean caverns, where thouſands are condemned to reſide, ſhut out from all hopes of ever again beholding the chearful light of the ſun, and obliged to toil out a miſerable life under the whips of imperious taſk-maſters. Imagine to yourſelf an hole in the ſide of a mountain, of about five yards over. Down this you are let, in a kind of bucket more than an hundred fathom; the proſpect growing ſtill more gloomy, yet ſtill widening, as you deſcend. At length, after ſwinging in terrible ſuſpenſe for ſome time in this precarious ſituation, you at length reach the bottom, and tread on the ground; which by its hollow ſound under your feet, and the reverberations of the echo, ſeems thundering at every ſtep you take. In this gloomy and frightful ſolitude, you are enlightened by the feeble gleam of lamps, here and there diſpoſed, ſo that the wretched inhabitants of theſe manſions can go from one part to another without a guide. And yet, let me aſſure you, that though they, by cuſtom, could ſee objects very diſtinctly by theſe lights, I could ſcarce diſcern, for ſome time, any thing; not even the perſon who came with me to ſhew me theſe ſcenes of horror.

From this deſcription, I ſuppoſe, you have but a a very diſagreeable idea of the place; yet let me aſſure you that it is a palace, if we compare the habitation with the inhabitants. Such wretches mine

 eyes

eyes never yet beheld. The blackneſs of their viſages only ſerves to cover an horrid paleneſs, cauſed by the noxious qualities of the mineral they are employed to procure. As they in general conſiſt of malefactors condemned for life to this taſk, they are fed at the public expence; but they ſeldom conſume much proviſion.——They loſe their appetites in a ſhort time; and commonly in about two years expire, from a total contraction of the joints of the body.

In this horrid manſion I walked after my guide for ſome time, pondering on the ſtrange tyranny and avarice of mankind, when I was accoſted by a voice behind me, calling me by name, and enquiring after my health with the moſt cordial affection. I turned and ſaw a creature all black and hideous, who approached me, with a moſt piteous accent, demanding, "Ah! Mr. Everard, don't you know me?" Good God! what was my ſurprize, when, through the veil of his wretchedneſs, I diſcovered the features of my old and dear friend Count Alberti! I flew to him with affection; and, after a tear of condolance, aſked how he came there? To this he replied, that having fought a duel with a general of the Auſtrian infantry againſt the emperor's command, and having left him for dead, he was obliged to fly into one of the foreſts of Iſtria, where he was firſt taken, and afterwards ſheltered, by

ſome

ſome banditti, who had long infeſted that quarter. With theſe he had lived for nine months, till, by a cloſe inveſtiture of the place in which they were concealed, and after a very obſtinate reſiſtance, in which the greateſt part of them fell, he was ſecured and carried to Vienna, in order to be broken alive on the wheel. When he arrived at the capital, he was quickly known, and, ſeveral of the aſſociates of his accuſation and danger witneſſing his innocence, his puniſhment of the rack was changed into that of perpetual confinement and labour in the mines of Idra. A ſentence, in my opinion, a thouſand times worſe than death.

As Alberti was giving me this account, a young woman came up to him, who, at once I ſaw had been born for better fortune. The dreadful ſituation of the place was not able to deſtroy her beauty, and even in this ſcene of wretchedneſs ſhe ſeemed to have charms to grace the moſt brilliant aſſembly.

This lady was daughter to one of the firſt families in Germany, and, having tried every means to procure her lover's pardon without effect, was at laſt reſolved to ſhare his miſeries, as ſhe could not relieve them. With him ſhe accordingly deſcended into theſe manſions, from which few ever return; and with him ſhe is contented to live, forgetting

the

the gaieties of life; with him to toil, despising the splendours of opulence, and contented with the consciousness of her own constancy.

I am, dear Sir,

Your's, &c."

Now can I tell all the feelings of your dear heart. Now see I your fancy busy with her magic pencil; and affecting is the picture it has begun. Begun—for your weeping eyes will not suffer you to finish it. Can not you through all your tears, distinguish Alberti and his wife dying in each others arms after about half a year? What a scene!

Is there any sum of money you would not give to have this tragedy end happily? That of course, is impossible. But Everard speaks of the poor souls in his next letter, which I may perhaps send you in *my* next.——

Come——be a good girl, and you shall have it now, though it will not give you much consolation.

"My

"My laſt to you was expreſſive, and perhaps too much ſo, of the gloomy ſituation of my mind. I own the deplorable condition of the worthy man deſcribed in it, was enough to add double ſeverity to the hideous manſions. At preſent, however, I have the happineſs to inform you, that I was ſpectaator of the moſt affecting ſcene I ever yet beheld. Nine days after I had written my laſt, a perſon came poſt from Vienna to the little village near the mouth of the greater ſhaft. He was ſoon after followed by a ſecond, and he by a third. The firſt enquiry was after the unfortunate Count; and I, happening to overhear the demand, gave them the beſt information. Two of theſe were the brother and couſin of the lady, the third was an intimate friend and fellow-ſoldier of the Count. They came with his pardon, which had been procured by the General with whom the duel had been fought, who was perfectly recovered from his wounds. I led them with all the expedition of joy down to his dreary abode, and preſented to him his friends, and and informed him of the happy change in his circumſtances. It would be impoſſible to deſcribe the joy that brightened up his grief-worn countenance; nor was the young lady's emotion leſs vivid at ſeeing her friends, and hearing of her huſband's freedom: ſome hours were employed in mending the appearances of this faithful couple, nor could I without a tear behold him taking leave of the former

wretched

wretched companions of his toil. To one he left his mattock; to another his working cloaths; to a third his little houſehold utenſils, ſuch as were neceſſary for him in that ſituation. We ſoon emerged from the mine, and he once again reviſited the ſight of the ſun, which he had totally deſpaired of ever ſeeing. A poſt-chaiſe was ready the next morning to take them to Vienna, whither, I am ſince informed by a letter from himſelf, they are returned. The empreſs has taken them into favour; his fortune and rank are reſtored; and he and his fair partner now have the pleaſing ſatisfaction of feeling happineſs with double reliſh, becauſe they once knew what it was to be miſerable."

Says not our friend Sterne, that the circumſtance of his being at Rennes at the very time the Marquis reclaimed his forfeited nobility and his ſword, was an incident of good fortune which will never happen to any traveller but a ſentimental one?—I believe it: and every other incident of good fortune befall all ſuch travellers!

Did not I ſay this ſecond part of the ſtory would not afford you *much* conſolation?

Excuſe

Excuſe me for ſuch a falſity. That was only to ſurprize you. Well I knew what would be my M.'s feelings.

Are you as deep in aſtrology as when you wrote laſt to me? On the page I have to ſpare I will ſend you ſome haſty lines which I ſcribbled the other day to ridicule the weakneſs of a Dr. W. who is as great a—fool at leaſt as Dryden, and never fails to caſt the nativity of his children.

Kind heaven has heard the parent's prayer,
Each goſſip hails the ſon and heir,
" Pray let the Doctor ſee."
" My maſter, ma'am? Your labour paſt;
" He's got among the ſtars, to caſt
" His ſon's nativity."

Three hours elaps'd, our ſage deſcends,
With " well, and how's the child, my friends?"
" He's happy, Sir, ere this."—
" Happy! why yonder ſtars ne'er ſhed
" Benigner influence on the head
" Of happier, I gueſs.
Worth, virtue, wiſdom, honour, wealth,
" Man's beſt and only riches, health,
" Aſſuredly await

" Heav'n's

"Heav'n's ſavour'd child——or never more
"Say I have knowledge to explore
"The ſecret page of fate.
"'Twas there I read my happy boy
"Full ſeventy ſummers ſhould enjoy
"Ere"—— when nurſe ſobb'd and ſaid,
"Good lack!——the babe, to whom kind heaven
"So many bounteous giſts hath given,
"Thoſe two hours hath been——dead."

LETTER XXXVII.

To the Same.

Ireland,
26 January 1777.

One of Lord Harcourt's ſuite will carry this to England. His Lordſhip was relieved from guard yeſterday by the arrival of the new Lord Lieutenant. As politicks have not much to do with love, I ſhall not trouble you with a hiſtory of the late reign, or with a prophecy of what will be the preſent. Only let our great actors take care they do not play the farce of America in Ireland.

My

My ſpirits, I thank you, are now tolerably well. But you know I am, at leaſt I know I have been ever ſince you have known me, a ſtrange comical fellow. Neither one thing nor t'other. Sometimes in the garret, but much oftner down in the cellar. If Salvator Roſa, or Rouſſeau, wanted to draw a particular character, I am their man. But you and I ſhall yet be happy together, I know; and then my ſpirits and paſſions will return into their uſual channels.

Why do you complain of the language and tenderneſs of my letters? Suppoſe they were not tender. What would you ſay, what would you think, then? Muſt not love ſpeak the language of love? Nay, do we not ſee every day that love and religion have mutual obligations, and continually borrow phraſes from each other? Put Jamie or Jenny, inſtead of Chriſt, and ſee what you will make of Mrs. Rowe's moſt ſolemn poems, or of Dr. Watts's hymns.

Let

Let me tranſcribe you a letter written by another perſon to a lady.

" Sir Benjamin telling me you were not come to " town at 3 o'clock, makes me in pain to know " how your ſon does, and I can't help enquiring af- " ter him and dear Mrs. Freeman. The biſhop of " Worceſter was with me this morning before I " was dreſſed. I gave him my letter to the Queen, " and he has promiſed to ſecond it, and ſeemed to " undertake it very willingly: though, by all the " diſcourſe I had with him (of which I will give " you a particular account when I ſee you) I find " him very partial to her. The laſt time he was " here, I told him you had ſeveral times deſired " you might go from me, and I have repeated the " ſame thing again to him. For you may eaſily ima- " gine I would not neglect doing you right on all oc- " caſions. But I beg it again for Chriſt Jeſus's ſake, " that you would never name it any more to me; " for, be aſſured, if you ſhould ever do ſo cruel a " thing as to leave me, from that moment I ſhall " never enjoy one quiet hour. And ſhould you " do it without aſking my conſent (which if I ever " give you may I never ſee the face of heaven!) I " will ſhut myſelf up, and never ſee the world " more, but live where I may be forgotten by " human kind."

What

What think you of this letter? If it ſhould have been written by a woman to a woman, ſurely you will allow H. to write a little tenderly to his own M. This was really the caſe. It is tranſcribed from "an account of the conduct of the Dowager Dutcheſs of Marlborough," printed for W. Smith in Dame-ſtreet, Dublin, 1742, which I bought at Wilſon's in Dame-ſtreet yeſterday. The pamphlet contains others as loving. This I find page 40. It was written to Lady Marlborough by her Miſtreſs (one would have thought the word *miſtreſs* in one ſenſe did belong to one of the parties) when ſhe was only Princeſs of Denmark. It refers to the quarrel between the Princeſs and her royal ſiſter and brother-in-law, becauſe ſhe would not part with her favourite, upon Lord Marlborough's having diſpleaſed the King.

Theſe two female lovers always correſponded, under the names of Mrs. Freeman and Mrs. Morley, at the particular deſire of the Princeſs, who fixed upon the names.

names. And this, after ſhe was Queen Anne.—Be aſſured, my M. that, although I write to you with almoſt the ſame madneſs of affection, I will ever imitate her example, for all its royalty, and exchange you for a muſhroom of your own raiſing (Mrs. Maſham).

LETTER XXXVIII.

To the Same.

Ireland, 6 Feb. 1777.

My laſt was merry, you know. I can't ſay as much for your laſt. To-day you muſt ſuffer me to indulge my preſent turn of mind in tranſcribing ſomething which was left behind her by a Mrs. Dixon, who poiſoned herſelf not long ſince at Inniſkillen. It was communicated to me by a gentleman, after a dinner yeſterday, who is come hither about buſineſs, and lives in the neighbourhood of Inniſkillen.

The unhappy woman was not above nineteen years of age. She had been mar-

ried

ried about two years, and lived with her husband all that time with seeming ease and chearfulness.

—She was remarkably chearful all the fatal day, had company to dine with her, made tea for them, in the evening, set them down to cards, retired to her chamber, and drank her cup of arsenick.

—She left a writing on her table, in which is obscurely hinted the sad circumstance which urged her impatience to this desperate act.

Enclosed is an exact copy even to the spelling.

"This is to let all the world know, that hears of me, that it's no crime I ever committed occasions this my untimely end; but despair of ever being happy in this world, as I have sufficient reasons to think so. I own 'tis a sinful remedy, and very uncertain to seek happiness, but I hope that God will forgive my poor soul; Lord have mercy on it! But all I beg is to let none reproach my friends with it, or suspect my virtue or my honour in the least, though I am to be no more.

Comfort my poor unhappy mother, and brothers and sisters, and let all mothers take care, and never force

force a child as mine did me: but I forgive her, and hopes God will forgive me, as I believe ſhe meant my good by my marriage.

Oh! that unfortunate day I gave my hand to one, whilſt my heart was another's, but hoping that time and prudence would at length return my former peace and tranquillity of mind, which I wanted for a long time: but oh! it grieves me to think of the length of eternity; and the Lord ſave me from eternal damnation! Let no one blame Martin Dixon*, for he is in no fault of it.

I have a few articles which I have a greater regard for than any thing elſe that's mine, on account of him that gave them to me (but *he* is not to be mentioned)——and I have ſome well-wiſhers that I think proper to give them to.

Firſt, to Betty Balfour, my ſilver buckles; to Polly Deeryn, my diamond ring: to Betty Mulligan, my laced ſuit, cap, handkerchief and ruffles; to Peggy Delap, a new muſlin handkerchief not yet hemmed, which is in my drawer, and hope for my ſake thoſe perſons will accept of theſe trifles, as a teſtimony of my regard for them.

I would adviſe † Jack Watſon to behave himſelf in an honeſt and obedient manner in reſpect to his mother and family, as he is all ſhe has to depend upon now.

* Her huſband.

† Her brother.

I go

I now go in God's name, though againſt his commands, without wrath or ſpleen to any one upon earth. The very perſon I die for, I love him more than ever, and forgives him. I pray God grant him more content and happineſs than he ever had, and hopes he will forgive me, only to remember ſuch a one died for him.

There was, not long ago, ſome perſons pleaſed to talk ſomething againſt my reputation, as to a man in this town; but now when I ought to tell the truth, I may be believed: if ever I knew him, or any other but my huſband, may I never enter into glory; and them I forgive who ſaid ſo; but let that man's wife take care of them that told her ſo; for they meant her no good by it.

With love to one, friendſhip to few, and good will to all the world, I die, ſaying, the Lord have mercy on my ſoul; with *an advice to all people never to ſuffer a paſſion of any ſort to command them as mine did in ſpite of me.* I pray God bleſs all my friends and acquaintance, and begs them all to comfort my mother, who is unhappy in having ſuch a child as I, who is aſhamed to ſubſcribe myſelf an unworthy and diſgraceful member of the church of Scotland,

Jane Watſon,
otherwiſe Dixon."

My

My pen ſhall not interrupt your meditations hereon, by making a ſingle reflection. We both of us have made, I dare ſay, too many on it.—She too was *Jenny*, and had her Robin Gray.

LETTER XXXIX.

To the Same.

Ireland, 27 March, 77.

If you write as you wrote laſt week, I cannot bear this diſtance. Poſitively you muſt think of what I propoſed laſt month.

That I may not diſobey your commands this morning by writing too tenderly, I will tranſcribe you ſomething in return for the contents of your laſt. It is in a different ſtile, but full as capital. Tell me whether you don't think my French *Robin Gray* a good companion to your Engliſh one. The young Abbé who gave it me, aſſured me it is almoſt totally unknown even in France, Louis Petit (a friend of

Corneille)

Corneille) wrote it, who died in 1693. Do let me set you the task of translating it, when you will of course give Jeremiah leave to go and mind his own affairs.

Dès que *Robin* eut vu partir *Toinette*
Il quitta lá se soin de son troupeau,
Il jetta loin panetiere et houlette,
Et ne garda rien que son chalumeau.
Il lamenta plus fort qu'un *Jérémie*;
Il souhaita mille fois le trespas;
Et, dans son mal, il na'a d'autre soulas
Que d'entonner, sur sa flûte jolie,
Triste chanson, qui finit par, hélas!
C'est grand pitié d'estre loin de s'amie.

Ces derniers mots, sans cesser, il répéte,
Tantôt assis sur le bord d'un ruisseau,
Tantôt couché dessus la tendre herbette,
Tantôt le dos appuyé d'un ormeau,
Onc ne mena Berger si triste vie.
Du doux sommeil il ne fait plus de cas;
Plus qu'un Hermite il fait maisgres repas;
Dances et jeux ne lui plaisent plus mie,
Et dans sa bouche il n'a rien qu'un——helas!
C'est grand pitié d'estre loin de s'amie.

Il n'eſt berger qui ſon mal ne regrette ;
Et prés de lui bergeres du hameau
Viennent chanter, filant leur quenouillette,
Pour conſoler ce triſte paſtoureau.
Mais leur doux chant point ne le ſolatie,
Tant la douleur le tient dedans ſes lacs !
Pour ne les voir, les yeux tient toujours bas
Et, ſi leur dit, " laiſſex-moi, je vous prie ;'
Puis auſſitôt revient á ſon——helas !
C'eſt grand pitié d'eſtre loin de s'amie.

ENVOI.

Fills de *Cypris*, plus malin qu'une pie,
A conſoler *Robin* l'on perd ſes pas :
Toinette ſeule, avec ſes doux appas,
Le peut tirer de ſa melancholie :
Rends la lui donc ; car, après tout——hél
C'eſt grand pitié d'eſtre loin de s'amie.

LETTER XL.

To the Same.

Ireland, 20 April, 17

Now you ſee there are ſomethin
Dreams. But why is not your alar
letter more particular about your
pl

plaint? Do they nurſe you as tenderly as I would? Are they careful about your medicines? For God's ſake tell them all round what happened lately here to Sir William Yorke, the chief juſtice.

Sir William was grivouſly afflicted with the ſtone. In his ſevere fits he uſed to take a certain quantity of laudanum drops. On calling for his uſual remedy, during the moſt racking pains of his diſtemper, the drops could not be found. The ſervant was diſpatched to his apothecary; but, inſtead of laudanum drops he aſked for laudanum. A quantity of laudanum was accordingly ſent, with ſpecial charge not to give Sir William more than twenty-four drops. But the fellow, forgetting the caution, gave the bottle into his maſter's hand, who, in his agony, drank up the whole contents, and expired in leſs than an hour.

Why, my deareſt love, did you conceal your illneſs from me ſo long? Now, you may have revealed the ſituation of

your health to me too late. God forbid! —If I write more, I ſhall write like a madman. A gentleman takes this who ſails for England to-day. To-morrow or next day the Colonel will be here. If Lord S. as I have reaſon to expect, has influenced him to refuſe me leave of abſence, I will moſt certainly ſell out directly, which I have an opportunity to do. At any rate I will be with you in a few days. If I come without a commiſſion you muſt not be angry. To find you both diſpleaſed and ill, will be too much for your poor H. For my ſake, be careful. Dr. —— I inſiſt upon your not having any longer. His experience and humanity are upon a par. Poſitively you muſt contrive ſome method for me to ſee you. How can love like mine ſupport exiſtence if you ſhould be ill, and I ſhould not be permitted to ſee you! —But I can neither think nor write any more.

LETTER XLI.

To the Same.

Cannon Coffee-houſe,
Charing-Croſs, 4 May, 77.

Did you get the incoherent ſcrawls I wrote yeſterday and the day before? Your's I have this inſtant read and wept over. Your feeble writing ſpeaks you weaker than you own. Heavens, am I come hither only to find I muſt not ſee you! Better I had ſtaid in Ireland. Yet, now do I breathe the ſame air with you. Nothing but your note laſt night could have prevented me, at all hazards, from forcing my way to your bed-ſide. In vain did I watch the windows afterwards, to gather information from the paſſing lights whether you were better or worſe. For God of Heaven's ſake ſend me an anſwer to this.

LETTER XLII.

To Mr———.

A. 4 May, 1777,
3 a clock.

My dear miſtreſs bids me write this from her mouth—"Theſe are the laſt words I ſpeak. My laſt thoughts will be on you, my deareſt H. In the next world we ſhall meet. Live, and cheriſh my memory. Accept the contents of this little box. Be a friend to my children. My little girl."——

LETTER XLIII.

To the Same.

A. 4 May, 1777.
5 o'clock.

My dear Soul,

At the hazard of my life I write this to tell you Heaven has ſpared my life to your prayers. The unfiniſhed note, which my haſty maid—I can't go on.

Sir,

Sir,

My dear Miſtreſs bids me ſay, Sir, that her diſorder has taken a turn within this hour, and the phyſicians have pronounced her out of all danger.—Honoured Sir, I humbly crave your pardon for ſending away my ſcribble juſt now, which I am afraid has made you uneaſy; but indeed, Honoured Sir, I thought it was all over with my poor dear miſtreſs; and then, I am ſure I ſhould have broke my heart. For, to be ſure, no ſervant ever had a better, nor a kinder miſtreſs. Sir, I preſume to ſee your Honour to-morrow. My miſtreſs fainted away as ſhe began this, but is now better.

A. 6 a'clock.

LETTER XLIV.

To Miſs ——.

Cannon Coffee-houſe,
27 June, 1777,
5 o'clock.

As I want both appetite and ſpirits to touch my dinner, though it has been ſtanding before me theſe ten minutes, I can claim no merit in writing to you. May you enjoy that pleaſure in your delightful ſituation on the banks of the Thames, which no ſituation, no thing upon earth, can in your abſence afford me!

Do you aſk me what has lowered my ſpirits to-day? I'll tell you. Don't be angry, but I have been to ſee the laſt of poor Dodd. Yes, "poor Dodd!" though his life was juſtly forfeited to the laws of his country. The ſcene was affecting—it was the firſt of the kind I had ever ſeen; and ſhall certainly be the laſt. Though, had I been in England when Peter Toloſa was

deſervedly

deſervedly executed in February, for killing Duarzey, a young French woman with whom he lived. I believe I ſhould have attended the laſt moments of a man who could murder the object of his love. For the credit of my country, this man (does he deſerve the name of *man?)* was a Spaniard.

Do not think I want tenderneſs, becauſe I was preſent this morning. Will you allow yourſelf to want tenderneſs, becauſe you have been preſent at Lear's madneſs, or Ophelia's? Certainly not. Believe me (you *will* believe me, I am ſure)—I do not make a profeſſion of it, like George S. Your H. is neither *artiſte* nor *Amateur*—nor do I, like Paoli's friend and hiſtorian, hire a window by the year, which looks upon the Graſs-market at Edinburgh.

Raynall's book you have read, and admire. For its humanity it merits admiration. The Abbé does not countenance an attendance on ſcenes of this ſort by his writings, but he does by his conduct. And

I would ſooner take Practice's word than Theory's. Upon my honour Raynall and Charles Fox, notwithſtanding the rain, beheld the whole from the top of an unfiniſhed houſe, cloſe by the ſtand in which I had a place.

However meanly Dodd behaved formerly, in throwing the blame of his application to the chancellor on his wife, he certainly died with reſolution. More than once to-day I have heard that reſolution aſcribed to his hope that his friend Hawes, the humane founder of the humane ſociety, would be able to reſtore him to life. But I give him more credit. Beſides, Voltaire obſerves that the courage of a dying man is in proportion to the number of thoſe who are preſent——and St. Evremond (the friend of the French M.) diſcovered that *les Anglois ſurpaſſent toutes les nations á mourir.* Let me ſurpaſs all mankind in happineſs, by poſſeſſing my *Ninon* for life, and I care not how I die.

Some little circumſtances ſtruck me this morning, which, however you may refuſe

to

to forgive me for so spending my morning, I am sure you would not forgive me were I to omit.—Before the melancholy procession arrived, a sow was driven into the space left for the sad ceremony, nor could the idea of the approaching scene, which had brought the spectators together, prevent too many from laughing, and shouting, and enjoying the poor animal's distress, as if they had only come to Tyburn to see a sow baited.

After the arrival of the procession, the preparation of the unhappy victim mixed something disagreeably ludicrous with the solemnity. The tenderest could not but feel it, though they might be sorry that *did* feel it. The poor man's wig was to be taken off, and the night-cap brought for the purpose was too little, and could not be pulled on without force. Valets de chambre are the greatest enemies to heroes. Every guinea in my pocket would I have given, that he had not worn a wig, or that (wearing one) the cap had been bigger.

At

At laſt arrived the moment of death. The driving away of the cart was accompanied with a noiſe which beſt explained the feelings of the ſpectators for the ſufferer. Did you never obſerve, at the ſight or the relation of any thing ſhocking, that you cloſed your teeth hard, and drew in your breath hard through them, ſo as to make a ſort of hiſſing ſound? This was done ſo univerſally at the fatal moment, that I am perſuaded the noiſe might have been heard at a conſiderable diſtance. For my own part, I detected myſelf, in a certain manner, accompanying his body with the motion of my own; as you have ſeen people wreathing and twiſting and biaſſing themſelves, after a bowl which they have juſt delivered.

Not all the reſuſcitating powers of Mr. Hawes can, I fear, have any effect; it was ſo long before the mob would ſuffer the hearſe to drive away with his body.—

Thus ended the life of Dr. Dodd. How ſhocking, that a man with whom I have

eaten

eaten and drank, ſhould leave the world in ſuch a manner! a manner which, from familiarity, has almoſt ceaſed to ſhock us, except when our attention is called to a Perreau or a Dodd. How many men, how many women, how many young, and, as they fancy, tender females, with all their ſenſibilities about them, hear the ſounds, by which at this moment I am diſturbed, with as much indifference as they hear muffins and matches cried along the ſtreets! *The laſt dying ſpeech and confeſſion, birth, parentage, and education*—Familiarity has even annexed a kind of humour to the cry. We forget that it always announces the death (and what a death!) of one fellow being; ſometimes of half a dozen, or even *more*.

A lady talks with greater concern of cattle-day than of hanging-day. And her maid contemplates the mournful engraving at the top of a dying ſpeech, with more indifference than ſhe regards the honeſt tar hugging his ſweetheart at the top of "Blackeyed Sufan." All that ftrikes us is the ridiculous tone in which the halfpenny ballad-finger chants the requiem. We little recollect that, while we are fmiling at the voice of the charmer, wives or hufbands (charm fhe never fo wifely) children, parents, or friends, perhaps all thefe and more than thefe, as pure from crimes as we, and purer ftill perhaps, are weeping over the crime and punifhment of the darling and fupport of their lives. Still lefs do we at this moment (for the printer always gets the ftart of the hangman, and many a man has bought his own dying-fpeech on his return to Newgate by virtue of a reprieve)—ftill lefs do we afk ourfelves, whether the wretch, who, at the moment we hear this (which ought to ftrike us as an) awful found, finds the halter of death about his neck, and now takes the longing farewel, and now hears the horfes whipped and encouraged to draw from under him for ever, the cart which he now, now, now feels depart from his lingering feet—whether this

this wretch really deſerved to die more than we. Alas! were no ſpectator to attend executions but thoſe who deſerve to live, Tyburn would be honoured with much thinner congregations.

Still Cannon Coffee-houſe,

Well—I have made an uncomfortable ſort of a meal on tea, and now I will continue my converſation with you. *Converſation*—a plague on words, they will bring along with them ideas! This is all the converſation we muſt have together for ſome days. Have I deſerved the miſery of being abſent from my M.? To bring proofs of my love, would be to bring proofs of my exiſtence. They muſt end together. Oh M. does the chaſte reſolution which I have ſo religiouſly obſerved ever ſince I offered you marriage deſerve no ſmiles from Fortune? Is then my evil genius never to relent? Had I not determined to deſerve that ſucceſs which it is not for mortals

mortals to command, I ſhould never have ſtruggled with my paſſions as I did the firſt time we met after your recovery. What a ſtruggle! The time of year, the time of day, the ſituation, the danger from which you were hardly recovered, the number of months ſince we had met, the langour of your mind and body, the bed, the every thing——Ye cold-blooded, white-livered ſons and daughters of chaſtity, have ye no praiſes to beſtow on ſuch a forbearance as that? Yet when your ſtrength failed you, and grief and tenderneſs diſſolved you in my arms; when you reclined your cheek upon my ſhoulder, and your warm tears dropt into my boſom; then—who could refrain;——then——

What then, ye clay-cold hyper-criticks in morality;

Then—even then——"I took but one kiſs, and I tore myſelf away."

Oh that I could take only one look, at this moment!

Your laſt ſays *the ſun will ſhine*. Alas, I

ſee

o signs of it. Our prospects seem shut or ever.

'ith regard to the stage—— we will of it. My objections are not because ıbt your success. They are of a diffe- kind——the objections of love and acy. Be not uneasy about my selling The step was not so imprudent. t think you of orders? More than you know you have told me I have much religion for a soldier. Will you escend to be a poor parson's wife?

I shall write till to-morrow at this rate.

. E T T E R XLV.

To the Same.

7 July, 77.

ıce last night I have changed my mind ally changed it. I charge you not to Irs. Yates this morning. Write her your mind is changed. Never will I nt to be supported by your labours. Never,

Never, never ſhall your face, your perſon, your accompliſhments be expoſed for ſo much an hour. By the living God I will not forgive you if you do not give up all thoughts of any ſuch thing.

LETTER XLVI.

To the SAME.

Croydon,
20 Sept. 1777.

That you have taken to drawing gives me particular pleaſure. Depend upon it you will find it ſuit your genius. But, in truth, your genius ſeizes every thing. While your old friend is eating his corn, I ſit down to tell you this; which I would not ſay to your face, leſt you ſhould call it flattery. Though you well know flattery is a thing in which *we* never deal. My opinion of the great man's ſtile of painting, who condeſcends to improve you in drawing, is exactly your's. Poſterity will agree with us. The ſubjects you recommend to his pencil are ſuch as I ſhould have expect-ed from my M.'s fancy. While I walked my horſe hither this morning, two or three ſubjects of different ſorts occured to me. All of them would not ſuit his ſtyle. But I know one or two of them would not diſ-pleaſe you, if well executed. Some of them I will ſend you.——

Louis xiv. when a boy, viewing the battle of St. Anthony from the top of Cha-ronne. In 1650, I think.

Richard Cromwell, when the Prince de Conti, Conde's brother, told him in con-verſation, at Montpelier, without know-ing him, that Oliver was a great man, but that Oliver's ſon was a miſcreant for not knowing how to profit by his father's crimes.

Milton, when the idea firſt ſtruck him of changing his myſtery into an epic poem.

Demoſthenes declaiming in a ſtorm.

William the Conqueror, and his rebel-lious ſon Robert, diſcovering each other in a battle; after they had encountered hand to hand for ſome time.

Charles

Charles XII. tearing the Vizir's robe with his ſpur. And again, after lying in bed ten months at Demotica.

"——Though my mother could na ſpeak,
" She look'd in my face till my heart was like
to break."

The Abra Prior's Solomon,

" When ſhe, with modeſt ſcorn, the wreath return'd,
" Reclin'd her beauteous neck, and inward
mourn'd."

Our Elizabeth, when ſhe gave her Eſſex a box on the ear.

Chatterton's Sir Charles Bawdin, parting from his wife——

" Then tir'd out with raving loud,
" She fell upon the floor;
" Sir Charles exerted all his might,
" And *march'd* from out the door."

The Conference of Auguſtus, Anthony and Lepidus (you are deep in Goldſmith,
I know.)

I know.) Do you remember the ſcene? Equally ſuſpicious of treachery, they agreed to meet on a little iſland near Mutina. Lepidus firſt paſt over. Finding every thing ſafe, he made the ſignal.——Behold them, yonder, ſeated on the ground, on the higheſt part of a deſolate iſland, unattended, fearful of one another, marking out cities and nations, dividing the whole world between them; and mutually reſigning to deſtruction, agreeably to liſts which each preſented, their deareſt friends and neareſt relations.——Salvator Roſa would not make me quarrel with him for doing the back ground. Your friend, if any one living, could execute the figures.

Let me ſuggeſt one more ſubject.——Monmouth's decapitation, in the time of James ii. Hiſtory ſpeaks well of his face and perſon. The circumſtances of his death are theſe.——He deſired the executioner to diſpatch him with more ſkill than he had diſpatched Ruſſel. This only added

ded to the poor fellow's confusion, who struck an infectual blow. Monmouth raised his face from the block, and with a look (which I cannot describe, but the painter must give) reproached his failure.——By the turn of the head, the effect of the blow might be concealed, and left to fancy; who might collect it from the faces of the nearest spectators. —— The remainder of the scene is too shocking for the eye, almost for the ear.—But, I know not how, whenever I am away from you, nothing is too shocking for *me*.———Monmouth again laid down his head. The executioner struck again *and again*, to as little purpose; and, at last, threw down the axe. The sheriff obliged the man, whose feelings all must pity and respect, to renew his attempt. Two strokes more finished the butchery.

Were it possible to tear off this last subject without destroying half my letter, I really would. It will make you shudder too much. But, you see, it is not possible; and you prefer such a letter as this,

I know,

I know, to none. The paper only affords me room to ſay my horſe is ready. Every ſtep he carries me from you, will be a ſtep from happineſs.

LETTER XLVII.

To the Same.

5 February, 1778.

Oh! my deareſt M. what I have gone through ſince I wrote to you laſt night it is impoſſible for me to deſcribe. Thank God, you were not in town! Suffice it that my honor and life are both as you wiſh them. Now, mine of laſt night is more intelligible. How ſtrange, that the kindeſt letter almoſt you ever wrote me, ſhould come to me preciſely at the time I was obliged to make up my mind to quit the world, or, what is more, *much more*, to quit you! Yet, ſo it was.

The

The ſtory my letter mentioned, of a friend who had received ſuch an affront as no human being could away with, was my own. Your feelings agreed with me, I am ſure. Duelling is not what I defend. In general, almoſt always, it may be avoided. But caſes may be put, in which it can be avoided only by worſe than death, by everlaſting diſgrace and infamy. Had I fallen, I know where my laſt thoughts would have lingered; and you and your children would have had ſome token of my regard. Be aſſured the matter is for ever at an end, and at an end as properly as even you can wiſh. How happy ſhall we be, in 79, or 80 (for before that time we ſhall ſurely be bleſt with each other!), to have thoſe friends about us who were privy to this day; and to talk over the poſſibility of it!

H. in all thy future life ſacred be every fifth of February!

My mind is too much agitated to write any more this evening. To-morrow I will be more particular. My laſt I am ſure

ſure could not alarm you; though, had any thing happened, it would have prepared you. Don't be alarmed by this. Upon my honour! (with which you know I never preface a falſity) I am not hurt; nor, as it ſince turns out, is the other gentleman—at leaſt not materially.

One trifling circumſtance I muſt mention. As I was determined either to kill or be killed (unleſs ſufficient apologies ſhould be made),—*the only proper, and leaſt pernicious idea of duelling*,—I did not ſee why I ſhould not recruit my ſtrength as much as poſſible. So about three o'clock, I took ſome cold ſaddle of mutton and brandy and water at my friend's. After which I went home to ſeal up ſome things for you, where my friend was to call for me. When I ſaw him coming to my door between 4 and 5, I had juſt wrung the affectionate hand of the man I moſt value, and committed to his care you and your dear little girl, and my dear ſiſter, &c. &c. Love, honour, revenge, and all my various feelings would,

in spite of myself, parch my tongue. As I took my hat out of my dressing-room, I filled a wine-glass of water, and drank half of it, to moisten my mouth. When I saw that glass again, about an hour ago, on returning to that home, which I never again thought to see, in order to write to her of whom I thought I had taken my last leave in this world—when I took that glass again into my hand, recollected my feelings on setting it down, and emptied the remainder of its contents, a libation of gratitude to the superintending Providence of Heaven—Oh M. no pen, not even your's, can paint my feelings!

Only remember—in all our future life, each fifth of February be ever sacred!

LETTER XLVIII.

To the Same.

—— street,
2 March, 1778.

Your going out of town so suddenly has not served to mend my spirits, but I will be as merry as I can. Were I to be *very* miserable after my late miraculous adventure, I should be guilty of *sullenness* against Providence. The minute account I gave you of it last week, was, I assure you, dictated to my pen by my feelings, before they had forgotten the affecting circumstances. Your observations are truly just and striking. Unpardonable as the affront which I had received appears to mortal eyes, I should not readily, I fear, have found an answer to the question of the enquiring angel, on entering the world of spirits, "What brings you hither?"

Did I tell you o'Saturday the particulars of the poor fellow who suffered this day ſe'nnight for murdering Mrs. Knightly? They are ſingular. He was an Italian, I underſtand. Such a thing is not credible, but of an Italian.

Mrs. Knightly's account was, that on the 18th of January Ceppi came into her room, ſhe being in bed, locked the door, ſat himſelf in a chair; and told her he was come to do her buſineſs. She, not underſtanding this, aſked him to let her get out of bed; which he did. He then took from his pocket two piſtols. She went towards the door in order to get out; but he ſet his back againſt it. She, to appeaſe him, told him he might ſtay breakfaſt. He anſwered he would have none, but would give her a good one. She then called out to alarm the houſe, ran towards the bed, and ſaid, "pray, don't ſhoot me!" and drew up cloſe to the curtains. He followed, and diſcharged the piſtol; after which he threw himſelf acroſs the bed, and fired the other piſtol at himſelf, which did not take effect. During this, a waſherwoman ran up ſtairs, and

and with a poker broke the bottom pannel of the door, through which Mrs. Knightly was drawn half-naked, and Ceppi, following, ran down ſtairs; but was purſued and taken. In his defence, he ſaid, he had propoſed honourable terms of marriage to her, but that ſhe had refuſed and deſerted him; that he was overcome with grief and love, and that his deſign was not to hurt her, but to ſhoot himſelf in her preſence.

It appears, I am afraid, from all the circumſtances, that, whatever his deſpair meant with regard to his own life, he certainly was determined to take away her's. How unaccountably muſt nature have mixed him up! Beſides the criminality and brutality of the buſineſs, the folly of it ſtrikes *me*. What—becauſe the perſon, on whom I have fixed *my* affections, has robbed me of happineſs by withdrawing *her's*, ſhall I let her add to the injury, by depriving me of exiſtence alſo in this world, and of every thing in the next? In my opinion, to run the chance of being murdered by the new object of her affections, or of murdering him, is as little reconcilable to common ſenſe as to common religion. How much leſs ſo to commit complicated murder, which muſt cut off all hopes in other worlds!

Yet, could I believe (which I own I cannot, from the evidence in this caſe), that the idea of deſtroying her never ſtruck him till his finger was at the trigger—that his only intention was to lay the breathleſs body of an injured lover at her feet—Had this been the fact, however I might have condemned the deed, I certainly ſhould have wept over the momentary phrenzy which committed it. But, as nothing appears to have paſt which could at all make him change his plan, I muſt (impoſſible as it ſeems) ſuppoſe him to have deliberately formed ſo diabolical a plan—and muſt rejoice that he was not of the ſame country, while I lament that he was of the ſame order of beings, with myſelf.

If the favour I mentioned to you o'Saturday be at all out of courſe, pray don't aſk it. Yet the worthy veteran I want to ſerve has now and then ſeen things happen not altogether *in* courſe. When he called this morning to learn how I had ſucceeded, I obſerved to him, while we were talking, that he got bald. "Yes," ſaid he, ſhaking his grey hairs, "it will happen ſo by people's continually ſtepping over one's head."

He little ſuſpected the channel of my application, but he aſked me this morning, whether 50l if he could ſcrape it together, properly ſlid into Miſs ——'s hand, might not forward his views. My anſwer was, that I had no acquaintance with the lady, but I knew *for certain* that ſhe had never in her life ſoiled her fingers with the ſmalleſt preſent of this ſort.

Happy, bleſt, to know you, to love you, and be loved by you!

LETTER XLIX.

To the Same.

Hockerill,
5 Sept. 1778.

Here did I ſit, more than two years ago, in this very room, perhaps in this very chair, thanking you for bliſs, for paradiſe; all claim to which I ſoon after voluntarily reſigned, becauſe I hoped they would ſoon be mine by claims more juſt, if poſſible, than thoſe of love. Two years.—how have I borne exiſtence all the while! But delicacy, and reſpect for you, enjoined forbearance. And hope led me on from day to-day, deceiving time with diſtant proſpects which I thought at hand. When will the tedious journey end? When will my weary feet find reſt? When ſhall I ſleep away my fatigues on the down-ſoft pillow of the boſom of love? Should hope continue to deceive me, you never ſhall make me happy, till you make me your huſband.

band. Yet, as we ſate upon the graſs, under the trees near the water, yeſterday, juſt before you returned me my ſtick, becauſe you thought the gentleman coming along the path by the mill was a certain perſon—yet, had I then looſened another button or two of my favourite habit, which was already opened by the heat; had I then (you remember, my Laura, the converſation and the ſcene) forgotten my reſolution, forgotten every thing, and riotted in all your glowing charms, which only love like mine could withſtand—who is he would dare to blame me? Who would dare to ſay I had done what he would not have done? But the ſcene muſt be ſhifted. —Sally Harris, you know, arrived only at the dignity of Pomona at Hockerill. Had my M. her due, mankind at large would admit her double claim to the titles of Minerva and of Venus.

To ſleep *here* is impoſſible. As well expect the miſer to ſleep in the place where he once hung in raptures over a hidden treaſure which is now loſt. This letter I have an opportunity to ſend to our old friend, for you, without taking it to town. Let me fill up the remainder of my paper with an almoſt incredible anecdote I learned from a gentleman who joined me on the road this morning, and travelled ſome miles with me. It happened laſt week I think. Peter Ceppi you remember. Surely that Providence which which prevents the propagation of monſters, does not ſuffer ſuch *monſtrous* examples as theſe to propagate.

One Empſon, a footman to Dr. Bell, having in vain courted for ſome time a ſervant belonging to Lord Spencer, at laſt cauſed the bans to be put up in church, without her conſent; which ſhe forbad. Being thus diſappointed, he meditated revenge; and having got a perſon to write a letter to her, appointing a meeting, he contrived to way-lay her, and ſurprize her in Lord Spencer's park. On her ſcreaming, he diſcharged a piſtol at her,

and

and made his eſcape. The ball wounded her but not mortally.

Oh love, love, can'ſt thou not be content to make fools of thy ſlaves, to make them miſerable, to make them what thou pleaſeſt! Muſt thou alſo goad them on to crimes! muſt thou convert them into devils!

LETTER L.

To the Same.

——— ſtreet,
28 Jan. 1779.

The ſhort note I wrote to you laſt night, immediately on my reaching town, you received, I hope. But why no anſwer to it? Why do you not ſay when we ſhall meet? I have ten thouſand things to tell you. My ſituation in Norfolk is lovely. Exactly what you like. The parſonage-houſe may be made very comfortable at a trifling expence. How happily ſhall we ſpend our time there! How glad am I that

I have

I have taken orders, and what obligations have I to my dear B. to Mr. H. and Dr. V.! Now, my happineſs can be deferred no longer. My character and profeſſion are, now, additional weights in the ſcale. Oh then, conſent to marry me directly. The day I lead you to the altar will be the happieſt day of my exiſtence.

Thanks, a thouſand thanks for your tender and affectionate letters while I was in Norfolk. Be aſſured G. could mean nothing by what ſhe ſaid. She is our firm friend, I am perſuaded. About an hour ago, I called there; but ſhe was out. Preſently I ſhall go again with this, in the hope of hearing ſomething about you.

Oh M.! every day I live I do but diſcover more and more how impoſſible it is for me to live without you.

Don't forget the 5th of next month. We *muſt* keep that day ſacred together.

LETTER LI.

To the Same.

—— ſtreet,
7 Feb. 1779.

While I live I will never forget your behaviour yeſterday. Were I to live an hundred years, I could never thank you enough. But your will be done.

The note I riſqued yeſterday you got, I hope. If you had not anſwered my laſt but one, I ſhould certainly have thrown this bundle of papers into the fire. Since you are now a good girl again, I ſend them to you. May they afford you any thing like entertainment! It was but laſt night I finiſhed them.—Adieu.—Much as I dread the expedition, to-morrow I believe muſt be the day.

17 February, 79.

LETTER LII.

To the Same.

At sea—20 February, 1

My dear little angel! I wrote my letter to you yesterday at 11 o'clock, when we sailed. I dined at two o'clo and, as for the afternoon, I had some r sic. I have my own servant on board 1 plays, and a couple of hands from Lon for the six weeks I am out. We wer good many at dinner. I had about n people yesterday, and shall have m when the rest of my squadron join They staid with me till near seven. I to supper about nine o'clock; but I co not eat, and so got to bed about 10. then prayed for you, my dearest lo kissed your dearest little hair; and down, and dreamt of you; and had on the dear little couch ten thousands tir in my arms, kissing you and telling how much I loved and adored you;

you ſeemeed pleaſed; but, alas, when I woke I found it all *dilluſion*—no body by me but myſelf at ſea. I roſe by time, at half paſt five, and went upon deck. There I found my friend Billy, and walked with him for about an hour, till Barrington came to me. We then breakfaſted about 8 o'clock, and by 9 I began and exerciſed the ſhips under my command till 12. It is now one, and when I finiſh this letter to you, my dear love, I ſhall dreſs and go to dinner at two o'clock. It is a rule on board to dine at 2, breakfaſt at 8, and ſup at 9—always, if nothing hinders me, I ſhall be a-bed by 10, or ſoon after, and up by half paſt five in the morning, in order to have, if there is any occaſion, orders ready for the fleet under my command before I begin to exerciſe them.—I am ſure the account of this day's duty can be no pleaſure to you, my love; yet it is exactly what I have done; and as I promiſed you always to let you know my motions and my thoughts, I have now performed my promiſe this day to

you,

you, and always will until the very laſt letter you ſhall have from me, which will be between 5 and 6 weeks hence. I ſhall ſend the Admiralty word that I am arrived at Spithead. Then I ſhall only wait for their anſwer, which will be with me in a few hours to ſtrike my flag——and then I ſhall return to you that inſtant. O' my love, mad and happy beyond myſelf to tell you how I love you and have thought of you ever ſince I have been ſeparated from you! The wind being contrary to-day about one, I put off dinner till three o'clock, in order to anchor ſhips for this this night in Portland road, juſt off Weymouth, about 2 miles. I hope to ſail to-morrow by 5 in the morning. I hope you are well. I am ſure I need not tell you I have had nothing in my thoughts but your dear ſelf, and long for the time to come back again to you. I will all the while, take care of myſelf becauſe you deſire, my dear little friend does, the angel of my heart! Pray do you take care of your dear

ſelf

ſelf for the ſake of your faithful ſervant, who lives but to love you, to adore you, and to bleſs the moment that he has made you generous enough to own him. I hope, my dear, nay I will dare to ſay, you never will have reaſon to repent it. The wind was not ſo contrary but we could have ſailed on: but I told Barrington that, as it was not fair, I would anchor, eſpecially as I could ſend one of my frigates in, for that I had diſpatches of conſequence to ſend to London. Indeed, my dear angel, I need not tell you. I know you read the reaſon too well that made me do ſo. It was to write to you, for God knows I have wrote to none elſe, nor ſhall I to any other but to the King. God bleſs you, moſt amiable and deareſt little creature living —aimons toujours, mon adorable petite amour.

Je vous adore plus que la vie meſme.

I have been reading for about an hour this morning in Prior, and find theſe few lines, juſt now applicable to us.

How

How oft had Henry chang'd his ſly diſguiſe,
Unmark'd by all but beauteous Harriet's eyes;
Oft had found means alone to ſee the dame,
And at her feet to breathe his am'rous flame;
And oft the pangs of abſence to remove
By letters, ſoft interpreters of love,
Till time and induſtry (the mighty two
That bring our wiſhes nearer to our view),
Made him perceive that the inclining fair
Receiv'd his vows with no reluctant ear;
That Venus had confirm'd her equal reign,
And dealt to Harriet's heart a ſhare of Henry's pain,

Such is my amuſement to read thoſe ſort of things that puts me in mind of our mutual feelings and ſituations. Now, God bleſs you, till I ſhall again have an opportunity of ſending to you. I ſhall write to you a letter a day as many days as you miſs *herein* of me when I do they ſhall all come Friday 16 June. God bleſs—I ſhan't forget you. God knows you have told ſo before I have your heart, and it lies warm in my breaſt. I hope mine feels as eaſy to you, thou joy of my life. Adieu.

Well,

Well, my M.—— how like you my pen to-day? Don't you think I am improved? In time I ſhall come to write ſuch letters as may appear in print. Were you not ſurpriſed to read a letter dated at ſea; and to find me write about my ſquadron, and the King, and the Lord knows what? when we parted but yeſterday within the bills of mortality.—Come, I'll now put off my maſk. The hopes you gave me yeſterday of ſo ſoon calling you mine, and to-day's uncommon fineneſs, had quite inſpired me with good ſpirits. A copy of the letter I have juſt tranſcribed was given me laſt night; and, as I promiſed to write to you to-day, I thought it would amuſe you more than any thing I could ſay. It has blood-royal in it, I aſſure you; and I'll take my *bible oath* of of its authenticity. When you have *nobody by you but yourſelf*, I think it will make you laugh. Compare this King's brother with my ſexton's ſon; who, during the compoſition

ſition of this letter, was writing Rowley's poems. Where I could make it ſenſe by ſtopping it, I have. The original is all written poſt. Cupid never ſtops to bait. Then he has no eyes, you know; which is an excuſe for bad ſpelling, and confuſion in the ſenſe. Poor blind boy! It's very well he can contrive to write at all. With regard to ſome of it, we are ſtill in the dark; but Lady G. made it out I dare ſay. Oh Love, almighty Love! with what eloquence does adoration of thee inſpire thy votaries!

Now, in my own character.—What you deſired ſo earneſtly ſhall certainly be done. As to the diſparity of our years, what you ſaid about it yeſterday did honour to your heart, but was all nothing to the purpoſe. My mind is made up. Beſides, I knew your age all along. Do you remember ſome ſufficiently bald poetry, with the reading of which I taxed your patience,

nce when I was quartered at * Hunt-
on, I believe? May I be hanged,
n, and quartered, if I did not, at the
I wrote it, know as well as yourself
many years you were older than I!
I well knew you were not acquainted
my age; which, by those lines, I
:d to conceal from you. Then I
ght, if you should suspect or come to
v I was younger than you, that though
dea (as you will see, unless you have
mitted them to the flames they merit)
s, in fact, upon our being *born* in the
e year, on the same day almost——
that you *might* take it to turn upon the
ımstance of our *birth-days* happening
ost together; and so overlook, in con-
ring the nearness of our birth-days, the
arity of our ages.

But

See Letter XVII. The Editor cannot but ob-
e, that if Mr. H. had not, in this subsequent
r, by the meerest accident in the world, ex-
ned those lines, they would have thrown an
ıst suspicion of suppositiousness on this whole
volume,

But it's uſeleſs to ſay a word more to me on this ſubject—all you pointed out I ſee—and I am determined. Remember *Ninon.* You are not quite old enough to be my *mother.*

By the day after to-morrow I hope to be able to tell you your buſineſs is done.—Of that ſong which I gave you ſome time ago, and with which you are often kind enough to treat me, I have diſcovered the author. You know what I mean—" When your beauty appears, &c." It was written by the elegantly-ſimple Parnell.

Let me to-day ſend you another, which, as I never heard you ſing it, I ſuppoſe you have never ſeen—otherwiſe, from what I know of your taſte, it muſt have been your favourite.

volume, and few people would have believed thoſe letters to have been genuine, from one of which it was ſo clear that H. was ſo very ignorant of Miſs ——'s age.

The

The moans of the forest after the battle of Flodden-field.

I have heard a lilting, at the ewes milking,
A' the lasses lilting before break of day;
But now theres a moaning, in ilka green loning,
Since the flowers of the forest are weeded away:

At bughts in the morning, nae blythe lads are scorning,
Our lasses are lonely, and dowie, and wae:
Nae daffing, nae gabbing, but sighing and sobbing.
Ilka lass lifts her leglin, and hies her away.

In

Lilting] Singing chearfully, with a brisk lively air, in a style peculiar to the Scots; whose music, being composed for the bagpipe, jumps over the discordant notes of the 2d and 7th, in order to prevent the jarring which it would otherwise produce with the drone or bass, which constantly sounds an octave to the key note. Hence this kind of composition is commonly stiled a Scotch *lilt*.—' *A'*] All.—' *Ilka*] Each.—' *Loning*] Lane; a word still in use in the northern parts. The word *green* is peculiarly emphatical; grown over with grass, by not being frequented.—' *Bughts*] Circular folds, where the ewes are milked——' *Scorning*] Bantering, jeering.—' *Dowie*] Dowly, solitary.—' *Wae*] Full of woe or sorrow.—' *Daffing*] Waggish sporting.—' *Gabbing*] Jestingly prating, talking gibble-gabble.—' *Leglin*] Can, or milking-pail.—' *Swankies*]

In har'st at the ſhearing, nae ſwankies are jeering,
Our banſters are wrinkled and lyard and grey:
At a fair or a preaching, nae wooing, nae fleeching,
Since the flowers of the foreſt are weeded away.

At e'en in the glooming, nae youngſters are
roaming.
'Bout ſtacks with the laſſes at boggles to play;
But ilka laſs ſits dreary, lamenting her deary,
Since the flowers of the foreſt are weeded away.

Dool and wae fa' the order—ſent our lads to the
border!
The Engliſh for once by a guile won the day:
The flowers of the foreſt, that ſhone aye the fore-
moſt,
The pride of our land now ligs cauld in the clay!

We'll ha' nae mair lilting, at the ewes milking,
Our women and bairns now ſit dowie and wae:
There's nought heard but moaning in ilka green
loning,
Since the flowers of the foreſt are weeded away.

kies] Swains.—' *Banſters*] Bandſters, binders-up of the ſhaves.—' *Lyard*] Hoary: being all old men. —' *A preaching*] A preaching in Scotland is not unlike a country fair.—' *Fleeching*] Fawning, flattering—' *Glooming*] Glimmering, twilight.—Do you remember Chatterton's note on *glommed*, in my letter about him?—' *Dool*] Dolour, ſorrow.—' ' *Wae fa'*] Woe befal, evil betide.—' *Ligs*] Lies.'

LETTER

LETTER LIII.

To the Same.

24th February, 1779.

Since we parted yeſterday I have thought a good deal of what we talked about. Though I did not promiſe to write to you till to-morrow, I take up my pen you ſee this morning. The buſineſs that is to forward our marriage (which can alone make me happy, and remove that melancholy you obſerve) cannot be done till evening—ſo I may as well ſpend this morning in talking to you upon paper.

The manner in which you account for the ſelf-deſtructon of that moſt wonderful boy Chatterton is phyſical, I aſſure you, as well as ſenſible. Tiſſot, in his Eſſay on the Diſeaſes incident to Literary Perſons, ſtarts from ideas very much like yours, only they are wrapped up in harder words. You ſhall ſee:

I

When

When the mind, a long time occupied, has forcibly impressed an action upon the brain, she is unable to repress that forcible action. The shock continues after its causes; and, re-acting upon the mind, makes it experience ideas which are truly delirious: for they no longer answer to the external impressions of objects, but to the internal disposition of the brain, some parts of which are now become incapable to receive the new movements transmitted to it by the senses.

The brain of Pascal was so vitiated by passing his life in the laborious exercises of study, thought, and imagination, that certain fibres, agitated by incessant motion, made him perpetually feel a sensation which seemed to be excited by a gulph of fire situated on one side of him; and his reason, overpowered by the disorder of his nerves, could never banish the idea of this fiery abyss. Spinello painted the fall of the rebel angels, and gave so fierce a countenance to Lucifer, that he was struck with horror himself; and during the remainder of his life, his imagination was continually haunted by the figure of that dæmon, upbraiding him with having made his portrait so hideous. Gaspar Barlæus, the orator, poet, and physician, was not ignorant of these dangers. He warned his friend Hughens against them: but blind with regard to himself, by immoderate studies he so weakened his brain,

brain, that he thought his body was made of butter, and carefully ſhunned the fire, leſt it ſhould melt him; till at laſt, worn out with his continual fears, he leapt into a well. Peter Jurieu, ſo famous in theological diſpute, and for his commentary on the Apocalypſe, diſordered his brain in ſuch a manner that, though he thought like a man of ſenſe in other reſpects, he was firmly perſuaded his frequent fits of the cholic were occaſioned by a conſtant engagement between ſeven horſemen who were ſhut up in his belly. There have been many inſtances of literary perſons who thought themſelves metamorphoſed into lanterns; and who complained of having loſt their thighs.

No one can deny that Chatterton muſt have gone through as much wear and tear of the imagination as any perſon Tiſſot mentions. But I would give a good deal, were it poſſible for me never again to think about Chatterton, or about his death, as long as I live—for I never do without being miſerable.

What you let fall about the propenſity of the Engliſh to ſuicide, is not true; though a very popular idea. And yet I

will relate to you, in the words of another person, an inſtance of Engliſh ſuicide much more cool and deliberate than any you ever heard, I dare ſay. It is a fact, and happened in 1732.

Richard Smith, a book-binder, and priſoner for debt within the liberties of the King's-bench, perſuaded his wife to follow his example, in making away with herſelf, after they had murdered their little infant. This wretched pair were, in the month of April, found hanging in their bed-chamber at about a yard's diſtance from each other; and in a ſeparate apartment, the child lay dead in a cradle. They left two papers incloſed in a ſhort letter to their landlord, whoſe kindneſs they implored in favour of their dog and cat. They even left money to the porter who ſhould carry the incloſed papers to the perſon to whom they were addreſſed. In one of theſe the huſband thanked that perſon for the marks of frindſhip he had received at his hands; and complained of the ill offices he had undergone from a different quarter. The other papers, ſubſcribed by the huſband and wife, contained the reaſons which induced them to act ſuch a tragedy on themſelves and their offspring. This letter was altogether ſurpriſing for the calm reſolution, the good humour, and the propriety, with which

which it was written. They declared, that they withdrew themſelves from poverty and rags; evils that, through a train of unlucky accidents, were become inevitable. They appealed to their neighbours for the induſtry with which they had endeavoured to earn a livelihood. They juſtified the murder of their child, by ſaying, it was leſs cruelty to take her with them, than to leave her friendleſs in the world, expoſed to ignorance and miſery. They profeſſed their belief and confidence in an Almighty God, the fountain of goodneſs and beneficence, who could not poſſibly take delight in the miſery of his creatures: they therefore reſigned up their lives to him without any terrible apprehenſions; ſubmitting themſelves to thoſe ways, which, in his goodneſs, he ſhould appoint after death.—— Theſe unfortunate ſuicides had been always induſtrious and frugal, invincibly honeſt, and remarkable for conjugal affection.

This tragedy I have ſhown you, becauſe I think France, lively France, in whoſe language ſuicide is an *Angliciſm*, can ſupply me with an anecdote as authentic of ſomething ſtill more cool and more deliberate, ſince the motives to the crime (to which no motive can be ſufficiently ſtrong) were ſo much weaker.——

On the day before Chriſtmas-day, 1773, about eleven o'clock, two ſoldiers came to the Croſs-Bow Inn at St. Dennis, and ordered dinner. Bordeaux, one of the ſoldiers, went out and bought a little paper of powder, and a couple of bullets, obſerving to the perſon who ſold them to him, that St. Dennis ſeemed to be ſo pleaſant a place, he ſhould not diſlike to ſpend the remainder of his life there. Returning to the Inn, he and his companion paſſed the day together very merrily. One Chriſtmas-day they again dined as merrily, ordered wine, and about five o'clock in the afternoon, were found by the fire, on breaking open the door, ſitting on the oppoſite ſides of a table, whereon were three empty champaign bottles, the following will and letter, and a half crown. They were both ſhot through the head; two piſtols lay upon the floor. The noiſe of the piſtols brought up the people of the houſe, who immediately ſent for M. de Rouilleres, the commandant of the maréchauſſée at St. Dennis.

The

The will I translated myself from a formal copy, which was taken for a friend of mine at St. Dennis, in 1774.

The WILL.

A man who knows he is to die, should take care to do every thing which his survivors can wish him to have done. We are more particularly in that situation. Our intention is to prevent uneasiness to our host, as well as to lighten the labours of those whom curiosity, under pretence of form and order, will bring hither to pay us visits.

Humain is the bigger, and I, Bordeaux, am the lesser of the two.

He is drum-major of mestre de camp des dragons, and I am simply a dragoon of Belzunce.

Death is a passage. I address to the gentleman of the law of St. Dennis (who, with his first clerk as assistant, must come hither for the sake of justice) the principle, which, joined to the reflexion that every thing must have an end, put these pistols into our hands. The future presents nothing to us but what is agreeable——Yet that future is short, and must end.

Humain is but 24 years of age; as for me, I have not yet completed four lustres. No particular reason forces us to interrupt our career, except the

the diſguſt we feel at exiſting for a moment under the continual apprehenſion of ceaſing to exiſt. An eternity is the point of re-union ; a longing after which leads us to prevent the deſpotic act of fate. In fine, diſguſt of life is our ſole inducement to quit it.

If all thoſe who are wretched would dare to diveſt themſelves of prejudice, and to look their deſtruction in the face, they would ſee it is as eaſy to lay a ſide exiſtence as to through off an old coat, the colour of which diſpleaſes. The proof of this may be referred to our experience.

We have enjoyed every gratification in life, even that of obliging our fellow-creatures. We could ſtill procure to ourſelves gratifications : but all gratifications muſt have a period. That period is our poiſon. We are diſguſted at the perpetual ſameneſs of the ſcene. The curtain is dropped ; and we leave our parts to thoſe who are weak enough to feel an inclination to play them a few hours longer,

Two or three grains of powder will ſoon break the ſprings of this moving maſs of fleſh, which our haughty fellow-creatures ſtile the King of Beings.

Meſſrs. the officers of juſtice, our carcaſes are at your diſcretion. We deſpiſe them too much to give ourſelves any trouble about what becomes of them.

As

As to what we ſhall leave behind us—for myſelf, Bordeaux, I give to M. de Rouilleres, commandant of the maréchauſſee at St. Dennis my ſteel-mounted ſword. He will recollect, that, laſt year, about this very day, as he was conducting a recruit, he had the civility to grant me a favour for a perſon of the name of St. Germain, who had offended him,

The maid of the inn will take my pocket and neck-handkerchiefs, as well as the ſilk ſtockings which I now have on, and all my other linen whatever.

The reſt of our effects will be ſufficient to pay the expence of the uſeleſs law proceedings of which we ſhall be the ſubject.

The half crown upon the table will pay for the laſt bottle of wine which we are going to drink.

At St. Dinnis, Bordeaux.
Chriſtmas-day, 1773. Humain.

Of the following letter from Bordeaux to his lieutenant in the regiment of Belzunce, I have not ſeen the french; I cannot therefore anſwer for the tranſlation, which does not appear to have been done carefully. Another friend ſupplied me with it. You ſhall have it as I had it from him.

" Sir,

During my reſidence at Guiſe, you honoured me with your friendſhip. It is time that I thank you. You have often told me I appeared diſpleaſed with my ſituation. It was ſincere, but not abſolutely true. I have ſince examined myſelf more ſeriouſly, and acknowledge myſelf entirely diſguſted with every ſtate of man, the whole world, and myſelf. From theſe diſcoveries a conſequence ſhould be drawn: if diſguſted with the whole, renounce the whole. The calculation is not long. I have made it without the aid of geometry. In ſhort, I am on the point of putting an end to the exiſtence that I have poſſeſſed for near twenty years, fifteen of which it has been a burden to me; and, from the moment that I write, a few grains of powder will deſtroy this moving maſs of fleſh, which we vain mortals call the King of Beings.

" I owe no one an excuſe. I deſerted, that was a crime; but I am going to puniſh it; and the law will be ſatisfied.

" I aſked leave of abſence from my ſuperiors, to have the pleaſure of dying at my eaſe. They never condeſcended to give me an anſwer. This ſerved to haſten my end.

" I wrote to Bord to ſend you ſome detached pieces I left at Guiſe, which I beg you to accept. You will find they contain ſome well-choſen

ſen

ſen literature. These pieces will ſolicit for me a place in your remembrance.

"Adieu, my dear lieutenant! continue your eſteem for St. Lambert and Dorat. As for the reſt, ſkip from flower to flower, and acquire the ſweets of all knowledge, and enjoy every pleaſure.

"Pour moi, j' arrive au trou
"Qui n'echappe ni ſage ni fou,
"Pour aller je ne ſçais où.

"If we exiſt after this life, and it is forbidden to quit it without permiſſion, I will endeavour to procure one moment to inform you of it; if not, I ſhould adviſe all thoſe who are unhappy, which is by far the greateſt part of mankind, to follow my example.

"When you receive this letter, I ſhall have been dead at leaſt 24 hours.

With eſteem, &c.
Bordeaux."

Is there any thing like this in Engliſh ſtory?

If we exiſt after this life—Ah, my brave Bordeaux, that is the queſtion; and a queſtion which even you could not anſwer in the *negative.*

——There's

————————There's the reſpect
That makes calamity of ſo long life,
For who would bear the whips and the ſcorns o'th'
time,
The pangs of deſpiſed love,
(which I could never bear),
————————The law's delay,
The inſolence of office, and the ſpurns
Which patient merit of th'unworthy takes?
But that the dread of ſomething after death
Puzzles the will,
And makes us rather bear thoſe ills we have,
Than fly to others that we know not of.

The pains theſe two poor fellows took (or rather Bordeaux, for he ſeems to have been the principal) to prevent any trouble or uneaſineſs to their ſuvivors, lead me to reflect how very uniformly the contrary is the conduct of ſuicides with us. One would ſometimes almoſt fancy that they ſtudied how they might commit the abominable crime ſo as to be found by thoſe whom the diſcovery would moſt effect. Have they wives, children; It muſt be done ſometimes in their preſence, in bed with them; often in in their hearing; almoſt always in ſuch a manner that they may be the firſt ſpectators of it. Mr. Y. Lord F. Mr. S. Lord C. Mr. B. are cruel inſtances of this. Oh for omnipotence to call ſuch ſavages back to life, and chain them to the hardeſt taſks of exiſtence! Is not the crime of ſuicide ſufficient, without adding to it the *murder* of a heart-broken wife or child? Hence you may, perhaps, draw an argument that every ſuicide is a madman. For my part, I have no doubt of it; and if Humain had fallen into the hands of a friend leſs mad than Bordeaux, he might have lived to have fought another day.

And here ends a long, dull letter, about a ſhort, entertaining converſation (on your part at leaſt). Don't ſtay long out of town, or I ſhall write you *madder* notes than you received during the week I was at ——. When I think of you, I am mad —— What muſt I be when I have reaſon to think (or fancy ſo) that you don't think of me? G. is gone.

LET-

LETTER LIV.

To the Same.

1 March, 1779.

Though we meet to-morrow, I muſt write you two words to-night, juſt to ſay, that I have all the hopes in the world ten days, at the utmoſt, will complete the buſineſs. When that is done, your only objection is removed along with your debts; and we may, ſurely, then be happy, and be ſo *ſoon*. In a month, or *ſix weeks at furtheſt*, from this time, I might certainly call you mine. Only remember that my *character*, now I have taken orders, makes expedition neceſſary. By to-night's poſt I ſhall write into Norfolk about the alterations at *our* parſonage.—To-morrow.—G.'s friendſhip is more than I can ever return.

LETTER

LETTER LV.

To Charles——.Esq.

20 March, 1779.

Your coming to town, my dear friend, will anſwer no end. G. has been ſuch a friend to me, it is not poſſible to doubt her information.———What intereſt has ſhe to ſerve? Certainly none. Look over the letters, with which I have ſo peſtered you for theſe two years, about this buſineſs. Look at what I have written to you about G. ſince I returned from Ireland. She can only mean *well* to me. Be not apprehenſive. Your friend will take no ſtep to diſgrace himſelf. What I ſhall do I know not. Without her I do not think I can exiſt. Yet I will be, you ſhall ſee, a *man*, as well as a lover. Should there be a rival, and ſhould he merit chaſtiſement, I know you'll be my friend. But I'll have ocular proof of every thing before I believe.

Your's ever.

LET-

LETTER LVI.

To the Same.

6 April, 1779.

It ſignifies not. Your reaſoning I admit. Deſpair goads me on. Death only can relieve me. By what I wrote yeſterday, you muſt ſee my reſolution was taken. Often have I made uſe of my key to let myſelf into the A. that I might die at her feet. She gave it me as the key of love—Little did ſhe think it would ever prove the key of death. But the loſs of Lady H. keeps Lord S. within.

My dear Charles, is it poſſible for me to doubt G.'s information? Even you were ſtaggered by the account I gave you of what paſſed between us in the Park. What then have I to do, who only lived when ſhe loved me, but to ceaſe to live now ſhe ceaſes to love? The propriety of ſuicide, its cowardice, its crime—I have nothing

to

to do with them. All I pretend to prove or to difprove is my mifery, and the poffibility of my exifting under it. Enclofed are the laft dying words and confeffion of poor Capt. J. who deftroyed himfelf not long ago. But thefe lines are not the things which have determined me. There are many defects in the reafoning of them, though none in the poetry.—His motives are not mine, nor are his principles mine. *His* ills I could have borne. He told me of his inducement poor fellow! But I refufed to allow them. Little did I imagine that I fhould ever have inducements, as I now have, which I *muft* allow. Thefe extraordinary lines are faid to be his. Yet, from what I knew of him, I am flow to believe it. They ftrike me as the production of abilities far fuperior to his; of abilities fent into the world for fome particular purpofe, and which Providence would not fuffer to quit the world in fuch a manner.

Till within this month, till G's information, I thought of felf-murder as you think

of

of it. Nothing now is left for me but to leap the world to come. If it be a crime, as I too much fear, and we are accountable for our paſſions, I muſt ſtand the trial and the puniſhment. My invention can paint no puniſhment equal to what I ſuffer here.

Think of thoſe paſſions, my friend—— thoſe paſſions of which you have ſo often, ſince I knew Miſs ——, ſpoken to me and written to me. If you will not let me fly from my miſery, will you not let me fly from my paſſions? They are a pack of blood-hounds which will inevitably tear me to pieces. My careleſſneſs has ſuffered them to overtake me, and now there is no poſſibility, but this, of eſcaping them.— The hand of Nature heaped up every ſpecies of combuſtible in my boſom. The torch of Love has ſet the heap on fire. I muſt periſh in the flames. At firſt I might perhaps have extinguiſhed them——now they rage too fiercely. *If* they can be ſmothered, they can never be got under.

Suppoſe

Suppoſe they ſhould conſume any other perſon beſide myſelf. And who is he will anſwer for paſſions ſuch as mine?—At preſent, I am innocent.

Did you ever read D'Arnaud? Let me tell you a ſtory I found in him the other day. It made me ſhudder at the precipice on which I ſtand. It determined me to ſhut the adamantine gates of death againſt poſſibility.

Salvini, an Italian (no Engliſhman could commit his crime), in whoſe mind my mind diſcovered its relation, becomes intimate with Adelſon, an Engliſhman of fortune, at Rome. Salvini accompanies him to England, and is introduced by him to Mrs. Rivers and her daughter, his intended wife. Adelſon introduced a rival and a —— but you ſhall hear. Love, who had never before been able to conquer Salvini, now tyrannized over him, as cruelly as he has tyrannized over me. The tale is well worked up. Love leads his victim, by degrees, from one crime to another; till, at laſt, on the day fixed for Nelly's marriage with Adelſon, Salvini murders her, and endeavours to murder himſelf. The attendants preſerve him, a further victim to juſtice. He is committed to Newgate—condemned

to

to death. Adelson bribes a jailor to afford Salvini that opportunity to escape, which he twice refuses. He satisfies *human* justice by suffering at Tyburn. Adelson and Mrs. Rivers increase his crime, by dying of grief in consequence of it.*

Oh Charles—Charles—as yet thy H. is no Salvini. Nor will I murder any but

* When first I read this letter I had never heard of D'Arnaud. I now enquired for such a writer. Still I could not credit Mr. H. Who could believe that poor H.'s story should be related so many years before it happened, under the name of Salvini? But so it is. (Epreuves du sentiment, par M. D'Arnaud. Maestricht, 1774. Tome 3. 101.) The circumstance is so remarkable, that a note an hour long might be written upon it. If H.'s story be more complete than Salvini's, it does but show that Nature is a better writer than D'Arnaud. He yields, yet yields only to her pen; and even Nature appears to have borrowed from D'Arnaud.—"What a compliment!" the reader says——"What "a writer, to deserve such a compliment!" adds the Editor.

Before poor H. concludes this letter, there is an allusion to the most singular scene which Rousseau has so wonderfully painted. *La nouvelle Heloïse*, Lettre 17.

myself

myſelf.—As yet the devil has not tempted me to plunge my *Eloiſe* along with me into the unfathomable depths of deſtruction.—Take the lines I mentioned. They are too good for the bad cauſe they were written to defend.—My watch I have ſealed up for you: wear it for my ſake. Crop has been a faithful ſervant to me, accept of him; and when he is too old to carry you, let him have the run of your park. He once (how happy was I that day!)—he once bore the precious burden of her for whom I die. Already have I bid you ſolemnly farewel. It ſhall not be repeated. While I *do* live,

Your own

H.

Averſe from life, nor well reſolv'd to die,
Us'd but to murmur, I retain my breath—
Yet pant, enlarg'd from this dull world, to try
The hoſpitable, though cold, arms of death.

What future joys ſhould bid me wiſh to live?
What flattering dreams of better days remain?
What proſpect can obſcure exiſtence give,
A recompence for penury and pain?

Is

Is there an hope that o'er this unton'd frame
Awaken'd health her wonted glow ſhall ſpread?
Is there a path to pleaſure, wealth, or fame,
Which ſickneſs, languor, and remorſe can tread?

Then wherefore ſhould I doubt? what ſhould I
fear?
Why for a moment longer bear my grief?
Behold! my great deliverer is near!
Immediate as I wiſh, his prompt relief.

O inſtance ſtrange of free, but blinded will,
Diſcuſs'd ſo much, ſo little underſtood,
To bear the certainty of preſent ill,
Before the uncertain chance of ill or good!

But what that chance? Why, be it what it may:
Still 'tis a chance: and here my woes are ſure
Yet think theſe woes are ſorrows of a day,
While thoſe to all eternity endure.——

Think on the horrors of eternal pain!
Imagination ſtartles at the name;
Nor can impreſs upon the labouring brain
Duration endleſs ſtill, and ſtill the ſame.——

Well haſt thou ſaid—nor can it be impreſs'd.
Hath blind credulity that abject ſlave,
Who thinks his nothingneſs, for ever bleſs'd,
Shall hold eternal triumph o'er the grave?

When oceans ceafe to roll, rocks melt away,
Atlas and Ætna fink into the plain,
The glorious fun, the elements decay,
Shall man, creation's flimfieft work, remain?

What fhall remain of man?—this outward frame?
Soon fhall it moulder to its native duft——
Or haply that unbodied fubtle flame
Which occupies and animates the buft?

Let but a finger ache, the kindred foul
Its intimate alliance fhall perceive:
Let ultimate deftruction grafp the whole,
The foul immortal and unchang'd fhall live.

Stop but one conduit, and the tone is loft;—
But burft each pipe, and tear up every key,
Then fhall the decompofed organ's ghoft
Swell the loud peal of endlefs harmony.——

So fhall that quality, whofe powers arife
From various parts by niceft art arrang'd,
With every fhock they fuffer fympathize;
But after their deftruction live unchang'd.—

So much for argument—the legends vain
Of prieftly craft reach not th'ingenous mind—
Let knaves invent, and folly will maintain,
The wildeft fyftem that deludes mankind.

Did there exiſt the very hell they paint;
Were there the very heaven they deſire;
'Twere hard to chooſe, a devil or a ſaint,
Eternal ſing-ſong or eternal fire.

Ye idle hopes of future joys farewell!
Farewell ye groundleſs fears of future woe!
Lo, the ſole argument on which to dwell;
Shall I, or ſhall I not, this life forego!

I know the ſtorm that waits my deſtin'd head,
The trifling joys I yet may hope to reap,
The momentary pang I have to dread,
The ſtate of undiſturb'd, undreaming ſleep—

Then all is known—and all is known too well,
Or to diſtract, or to delay my choice:
No hopes ſolicit, and no fears rebel
Againſt mine ultimate, determin'd voice.

Had I ſuſpicions that a future ſtate
Might yet exiſt, as haply I have none—
'Twere worth the coſt, to venture on my fate,
Impell'd by curioſity alone.

Sated with life, and amply gratify'd
In every varied pleaſure life can give,
One ſole enjoyment yet remains untry'd,
One only novelty—to ceaſe to live.

Not

Not yet reduc'd a ſcornful alms to crave,
Not yet of thoſe with whom I liv'd the ſport;
No great man's pander, paraſite, or ſlave—
O Death, I ſeek thy hoſpitable port.

Thou, like the virgin in her bridal ſheet,
Seemeſt prepar'd, conſenting, kind, to lie;
The happy bridegroom I, with haſty feet,
Fly to thine arms in rapt'rous extaſy.

LETTER LVII.

To Mr. B——.

7 April, 1779.

My dear F.

When this reaches you I ſhall be no more, but do not let my unhappy fate diſtreſs you too much. I ſtrove againſt it as long as poſſible, but it now overpowers me. You know where my affections were placed; my having by ſome means or other loſt her's (an idea which I could not ſupport) has driven me to madneſs. The world will condemn me, but your heart will pity me. God bleſs you, my dear F. Would

I had a ſum of money to leave you, to convince you of my great regard! You were almoſt my only friend. I have hid one circumſtance from you, which gives me great pain. I owe Mr. W. of Goſport one hundred pounds, for which he has the writings of my houſes; but I hope in God, when they are ſold, and all other matters collected, there will be nearly enough to ſettle your account. May almighty God bleſs you and *your*'s, with comfort and happineſs; and may you ever be a ſtranger to the pangs I now feel! May Heaven protect my beloved woman, and forgive this act, which alone could relieve me from a world of miſery I have long endured! Oh! if it ſhould be in your power to do her any act of friendſhip, remember your faithful friend,

J. H.

LETTER LVIII.

To Charles ——, Esq.

Tothil-fields.
8 April, 1779.

I am alive—and she is dead. I shot her, and not myself. Some of her blood and brains is still upon my cloaths. I don't ask you to speak to me, I don't ask you to look at me. Only come hither, and bring me a little poison; such as is strong enough. Upon my knees, I beg, if your friendship for me ever was sincere, do, *do*, bring me some poison.

LETTER LIX.

To the Same.

9 April 79.

Your note just now; and the long letter I received at the same time, which should have found me the day before yesterday, have changed my resolution. The promiſe you deſire, I moſt ſolemnly give you. I will make no attempt upon my life. Had I received your comfortable letter when you meant I ſhould. I verily do not think this would have happened.

Pardon what I wrote to you about the poiſon. Indeed I am too compoſed for any ſuch thing now. Nothing ſhould tempt me. My death is all the recompence I can make to the laws of my country. Dr. V. has ſent me ſome excellent advice, and Mr. H. has refuted all my falſe arguments. Even ſuch a being as I finds friends.

Oh, that my feelings and his feelings would let me ſee my *deareſt* friend. Then I would tell you how this happened.

LETTER

LETTER LX.

To the Same.

Newgate,
14 April, 1779.

My best thanks for all your goodness ce this day se'nnight. Oh, Charles, s is about the time. I cannot write.

My trial comes on either Friday or Sa- rday. It will be indeed a trial. God hom I have so outraged) can alone tell w I shall go through it. My resolution not fixed as yet about pleading guilty: he arguments by which they tell me I ay escape that death so much my due, I rtainly will not suffer to be used. My esent situation of mind you may collect om the enclosed copy of what I mean to y, if I continue in the resolution, in hich I yesterday wrote you word I was, pleading not guilty.

" My Lord,

I ſhould not have troubled the Court with the examination of witneſſes to ſupport the charge againſt me, had I not thought the pleading guilty to the indictment would give an indication of contemning death, not ſuitable to my preſent condition; and would, in ſome meaſure, make me acceſſary to a ſecond peril of my life. And I likewiſe thought that the juſtice of my country ought to be ſatisfied, by ſuffering my offences to be proved, and the fact to be eſtabliſhed by evidence.

I ſtand here the moſt wretched of human beings! and confeſs myſelf criminal in a high degree. I acknowledge *with ſhame and repentance* that my determination againſt my owu life was formal and complete. I proteſt, with that regard to truth which becomes my ſituation, that the will to deſtroy her, who was ever dearer to me than life, was never mine until a momentary frenzy overcame me, and induced me to commit the deed I deplore.—The letter which I meant for my brother-in-law, after my deceaſe, will have its due weight, as to this point, with good men.

Before this dreadful act, I truſt, nothing will be found in the tenor of my life, which the common charity of mankind will not readily excuſe. I have no wiſh to avoid the puniſhment which the laws of my country appoint for my crime; but, being already too unhappy to feel a puniſhment in death,

death, or a satisfaction in life, I submit myself to the disposal and judgment of Almighty God, and to the consequences of this enquiry into my conduct and intention."

Whatever the world may think, you, I know, believe that I had no intention against her till the *very instant*. The account I wrote to you of the shocking business since it happened, was the real truth. All Tuesday, after I had finished my letter to you, I in vain sought for an opportunity to destroy myself in her presence. So, again, on the Wednesday, all the morning. In the afternoon, after dining at poor B.'s, I saw Lord S.'s coach pass by the Cannon Coffee-house, where I was watching for it. I followed it to G.'s (inhuman, and yet not guilty G.!) From her house I saw it take them to the play. Now, I was determined; and went to my lodgings, for my pistols, where I wrote a letter to B. which I put into my pocket, intending to send it; but, as I forgot it, the letter was found there. When I returned to

Covent-Garden, I waited for the conclusion of the play, in the Bedford Coffee-House. What a figure must I have been! Indeed, I overheard one gentleman say to a friend, that I looked as if I was out of my senses. Oh, how I wished for the play to be over! I had charged my pistols with the kindest letter she ever wrote me; a letter which made me the happiest of mortals, and which had ever since been my talisman. At last, arrived the end of the play, and the beginning of my tragedy. I met them in the stone passage, and had then got the pistol to my forehead, but she did not see me, (nor did any one, I suppose.) And the crowd separated us. This accident I considered as the immediate intervention of Providence. I put up my pistol, turned about, and should (I most firmly believe) have gone out the other way, and have laid aside my horrid resolution, had I not looked round and seen Mr. M. (whom I immediately construed into the favoured lover described by G.) offer her a hand, which I

thought

thought was received with particular pleasure. The ſtream of my paſſions, which had been ſtopped, now overwhelmed me with redoubled violence. It hurried me after them. Jealouſy ſuggeſted a new crime and nerved anew the arm of deſpair. I overtook them at the carriage, and——— and, at about the time I am now writing this, felt more than all the tortures of all the damned together.

What ſhall I not feel at the neceſſary recital of the tragedy, at my trial!

LETTER LXI.

To Mr. ———, in Newgate,

17 April, 79.

If the murderer of Miſs ——— wiſhes to live, the man he has moſt injured will uſe all his intereſt to procure his life.

grateful to thy goodness, to be thought unworthy thy presence, to be driven from the light of thy countenance.

Well thou knowest I could not brook the thoughts of wanting gratitude to things beneath me in the creation; to a dog, a horse: almost to things inanimate; a tree, a book. And thinkest thou that I could bear the charge of want of gratitude to thee!

And, might—O might I resign the joys of the other world, which neither eye can see, nor tongue can speak, nor imagination dream, for an eternal existence of love and bliss with her, whom——

Presumptuous murderer! The bliss you ask were paradise.——

My father, who art in heaven, I bow before thy mercy; and patiently abide my sentence.

These papers which will be delivered to you after my death, my dear friend, are not letters. Nor know I what to call them. They will exhibit, however, the picture of a heart which has ever been your's more than any other man's.

How have I seen the poor soul affected at that recitative of Iphis in her favourite Jephtha!

"Ye

"Ye ſacred prieſts, whoſe hands ne'er yet were
ſtained
"With human blood!"

To think that I ſhould be her prieſt, her murderer! In one of her letters ſhe tells me, I recollect, that ſhe could die with pleaſure by my hand, ſhe is ſure ſhe could. Poor ſoul! Little did ſhe think——

It is odd, but I know for a certainty that this recitative and the air which follows it, "Farewel, &c." were the laſt words ſhe ever ſung. Now I muſt ſay, and *may* ſay, *experimentally*——

"Farewell, thou buſy world, where reign
"Short *hours* of joy, and *years* of pain!"
I *may not* add——
"Brighter ſcenes I ſeek above,
"In the realms of peace and *love*."

Love! gracious God, this word in this place, at this time!

Oh!

Newgate, Sunday, 18 April, 79.
4 in the morning.

O, Charles, Charles—torments, tortures! Hell, and worse than hell!

When I had finished my last scrap of paper, I thought I felt myself composed, resigned. Indeed, I was so——I am so now.

I threw my wearied body—wearied, Heaven knows, more than any labourer's, with the workings of my mind—upon the floor of my dungeon.

Sleep came uncalled, but only came to make me more completely cursed.

This world was past, the next was come; but, after that, no other world. All was revealed to me. My eternal sentence of mental misery (from which there was no flight) of banishment from the presence of my father, of more than poetry e'er feigned or weakness feared, was past, irrevocably past.

Her verdict too of punishment was pronounced, Yes, Charles—she, she was punished—and by whose means punished?

Even in her angel mind were failings, which it is not wonderful I never saw, since Omniscience, it seemed, could hardly discern them. O, Charles, these foibles, so few, so undiscernible, were still, I thought in my dream, to be expiated. For my hand

hand sent her to heaven before her time, with all her few foibles on her head.

Charles, I saw the expiation—these eyes beheld her undergo the heavenly punishment.

That past, she was called, I thought, to the reward of her ten thousand virtues.

Then, in very deed, began my hell, my worse than woman ever dreamed of hell. Charles, I saw her, as plainly as I see the bars of my dungeon, through which the eye of day looks upon me now for almost the last time. Her face, her person were still more divine than when on earth—they were cast anew, in angel moulds. Her mind too I beheld, as plainly as her face; and all its features. That was the same—that was not capable of alteration for the better.

But, what saw I else? That mind, that person, that face, that angel—was in the bosom of another angel. Between us was a gulph, a gulph impassible! I could not go to her, neither could she come to me.

No—nor did she wish it. There was the curse.

Charles, she saw me, where I was, steeped to the lips in misery. She saw me; but without a tear, without one sigh.

One sigh from her, I thought—and I could have borne all my sufferings.

A sigh, a tear! She smiled at all my sufferings. Yes, she, even she, enjoyed the tortures, the wrackings of my ſoul. She bade her companion angel too enjoy them. She ſeemed to feaſt upon my griefs; and only turned away her more than damning eyes, to turn them on her more than bleſt companion.

Flames and brimſtone—corporal ſufferance—were paradiſe to ſuch eternal mental hell as this.

Oh! how I rejoiced, how I wept, ſobbed with joy, when I awoke, and diſcovered it was only a dream, and found myſelf *in the condemned cell of Newgate.*

Mr. H. and Dr. V. neither of whom you know, I believe, are exceedingly kind to me. The latter writes to me, the former ſees me, continually. Your poor H. finds more friends than he merits.

Among my papers you will ſee ſome lines I wrote on reading *Goethe's** "Werther," tranſlated from German into French, which, while I was in Ireland,

* Extract from the French Tranſlator's preface to Werther.

(Werther, traduit de l'Allemande, Maeſtricht. 1776. Second partie, p. 229.)

Jeune homme ſenſible! quand tu éprouveras la premiere atteinte de la plus violente des paſſions pour un objet qui ne peut être à toi, tu diras: tel étoit

And ſhould the affecting page be haply read
By ſome new Charlotte, mine will then be dead—
(Yes, ſhe ſhall die—ſole ſolace of my love!
And we ſhall meet, for ſo ſhe ſaid, above)—
O, Charlotte, M———, by whatever name
Thy faithful Werther hands thee down to fame—
O be thou ſure thy Werther never knows
The fatal ſtory of my kindred woes!
O do not, fair one—by my ſhocking end
I charge thee!—do not let thy feeling friend
Shed his ſad ſorrows o'er my tearful tale:—
Example, ſpite of precept, may prevail.

Nay, much loved M. though a fond deſire
To prove thy huſband, prove thy childrens' ſire;
Tho' theſe, and other duties, thou muſt know,
Would hold his hand from death's forbidden blow—

fortuné encore, peut-être la vertu s'éloignera de mon cœur; je chercherai á ſéduire cette femme; and ſi mes efforts ſont vains, je maſſacrerai ſon époux—*elle même*—Fuyons! évitons le crime, ou l'infortune: allons chercher dans d'autres climats l'oubli d'un objet trop dangereux, & la jouiſſance de plaiſirs moins funeſtes.

And yet, *Elle même* had no effect on H.

Yet

Yet might my gloomy tale full surely shroud
His brightest day in melancholy's cloud;
Yet might thy H. lead, to his last breath
A life more shocking than even Werther's death.

Newgate, Sunday, 18 April, 79,
5 o'clock in the afternoon.

Since I wrote to you this morning I have more than once taken up my pen. For what can I do, which affords me more pleasure than writing to such a friend as you are, and have been, to me?

Pleasure! Alas, what business has such a wretch as I with such a word as that? However, pouring myself out to you thus upon paper is, in some measure, drawing off my sorrows——it is not thinking.

Cruel G.! And yet I can excuse her. She knew not of what materials I was made. Lord S. wished to preserve a treasure which any one would have prized. G. was employed to preserve the treasure. And she suspected not that my soul, my existence, were wrapped up in it.

O, my dear Charles, that you could prevail upon yourself to visit this sad place! And yet—our mutual feelings would render the visit useless. So ——it is better thus.

Now

Now, perhaps, you are enjoying a comfortable and happy meal. There, again, my misfortunes! Of happineſs and comfort, for the preſent, I have robbed you. H. has murdered happineſs.

But this is the hour of dinner. How many are now comfortable and happy? While I——

How many, again, with every thing to make them otherwiſe, are, at this moment, miſerable!

The meat is done too little, or too much—(Should the pen of fancy ever take the trouble to invent letters for me, I ſhould not be ſuffered to write to you thus, becauſe it would ſeem *unnatural*. Alas—they know not how gladly a wretch like me forgets himſelf)—The ſervant, I ſay, has broken ſomething—ſome *friend* (as the phraſe is) does not make his promiſed appearance, and conſequently is not eye-witneſs of the unneceſſary diſhes which the family pretends to be able to afford—or ſome *friend* (again) drops in unexpectedly, and ſurprizes the family with no more diſhes upon the table than are neceſſary.

Ye home-made wretches, ye ingenious inventors of ills, before ye ſuffer yourſelves to be ſoured and made miſerable, for the whole remainder of this Sunday, by ſome trifle or another, which does not deſerve the name of accident, look here—behold, indeed, that miſery of which your diſcontentedneſs complains!

Peep

Peep through the grate of this my only habitation, ye who have town-houses and country-houses. Look into my soul—recollect in how few hours I am to die, die in what manner, die for what offence;

Now, go, be cross and quarrel with your wives, or your husbands, or your children, or your guests—begin to curse and to swear—and call Almighty God to witness that you are the most miserable, unlucky, wretches upon the face of the earth—because the meat is roasted half a dozen turns too much, or because your cooks have not put enough of seasoning into your pies.

I was obliged to lay down my pen. Such a picture as this, in which myself made the principal figure, was rather too much.

Good God!—to look back over the dreadful interval between to-day and last October two years. What a tale would it make of woe! Take warning from me, my fellow creatures, and do not love like H.

Still, Sunday.
7 o'clock.

When these loose, incoherent papers shall come into your hands after my death, it will afford you some consolation to know my temper of mind at last.

Charles, as the awful moment approaches, I feel myself more, and more, and more, composed, and calm, and resigned.

It always, you know, was my opinion, that man could bear a great load of affliction better than a small one. I thought so then—now I am sure of it. This day se'nnight I was mad, perfectly mad. This afternoon I am all mildness.

This day se'nnight!—To look back is death, is hell. 'Tis almost worse than to look forward.

Let me endeavour to get out of myself.

In proof of that opinion which you always ridiculed—go to the gaming table—observe that adventurer, who is come with the last fifty he can scrape together. See—how he gnashes his teeth, bites his fists, and works all his limbs! He has lost the first throw—his 50 are reduced to 40. Observe him now—with what composure his arms are wrapped about him! What a smooth calm has suddenly succeeded to that dreadful storm which so lately

lately tore up his whole countenance! Whence the reason think you? Has fortune smiled on him? —Directly the contrary. His 40 are now dwindled away to five. His all, nay more, his very existence, his resolution to live or die, depend upon this throw. Mark him—how calmly, how carelessly he eyes the box. I am not sure he does not almost wish to lose, that he may defy ill-luck, and tell her she has done her worst.

See——

—On a moment's point, th' important dye
Of life and death spins doubtful ere it falls,
And turns up—death.

I'll surrender my opinion for untenable, if a common observer, from his countenance, would not rather point him out as the winner, than the agitated person yonder who really has won.

——Since I wrote what you last read, I caught myself marching up and down my cell with the step of haughtiness; hugging myself in my two arms; and muttering between my grating teeth, "What a *compleat wretch* I am!"

But—is there not a God! Did not that God create me? Does not that God know my heart, my whole heart? Oh! yes, yes, yes!

To-morrow then—And let to-morrow come—I am prepared.

God

God (who knows my heart, and will judge me, I trust, by that heart) knows it is not with a view to diminish my own guilt, the magnitude and enormity whereof I acknowledge—but—let not those, who survive me, flatter themselves that all the guilt of mankind goes to the grave, to the gallows (gracious heaven) with H.

I shall leave behind me culprits *of the same kind as myself*—culprits who will not make my trifling atonement of an ignominious death. Oh may they see their crimes, and weep over them before they are confronted with the injured parties at the footstool of the throne of the God of heaven!

These are crimes (as indeed are all the crimes of men, however noiseless or inaudible) with which the listening angel flies up to heaven's chancery—but these are not they upon which the recording angel drops a tear as he notes them down. The pencil of eternity engraves such crimes as these on adamantine tablets, which shall endure to the end of time. Mine, mine, perhaps, may head the list.

Be merciful, O God! be merciful!

Reflexion in this world is almost worse than the worst which offended Omnipotence can inflict upon me in the next. I must fly from it.

And

And are there not crimes as bad as mine? It is little my intention to argue away the badness of my crime—but there surely are, and worse.

Let that gallant, gay, young gentleman yonder hold up his hand. Yes, sir—you I first arraign. Not for breach of friendship, not for false oaths to credulous virgins, not for innocence betrayed—these are no longer crimes; these are the accomplishments of our age. Sir, you are indicted for slow and deliberate murder.—Put not on that confident air, that arrogant smile of contempt and defiance. Demand not with a sneer to have the witnesses produced who were present when you struck the stroke of death. Call not aloud for the blood-stained dagger, the dry-drawn bowl, the brain-splashed pistol. Are these the only instruments of death? You know they are not. Murder is never at a loss for weapons.

Sir, produce your wife.——See, see!—what indignation flashes in his eyes! A murderer, and the murderer of his wife! May the calumniator—! —Sir, no imprecations, no oaths; those are what betrayed that wife. You did not plant a dagger in her breast; but you planted there grief, disease, death. She, sir, who gave you all, was destroyed, was murdered by your ill usage. And not suddenly, not without giving her time to know what was to happen. She saw the lingering stroke, she perceived the impossibility to avoid it; she felt it tenfold from the hands of a much-loved husband.

Were theſe ſcraps of paper to be ſeen by any other eye than your's, common people would wonder that, in proportion as the moment drew nearer, I got further and further from myſelf. It may be contrary to the rules of criticks, but ſo it is.—To think, or to write about myſelf, is death, is hell. My feelings will not ſuffer me to date theſe different papers any more.

Let me pay a ſmall tribute of praiſe—How often have you and I complained of familiarity's blunting the edge of every ſenſe on which ſhe lays her hand? At her bidding, beauty fades even in the eyes of love; and the ſon of pity ſmiles at ſorrow's bleeding breaſt. In her preſence, who is he that ſtill continues to behold the ſcene of delight, or that ſtill hears the voice of mourning? What then is the praiſe of that gaoler, who in the midſt of miſery, and crimes, and death, ſets familiarity at defiance, and ſtill preſerves the feelings of a man? The author of the life of *Savage* gives celebrity to the Briſtol gaoler, by whoſe humanity the latter part of that ſtrange man's life was rendered more comfortable. Shall no one give celebrity to the preſent keeper of Newgate? Mr. Akerman marks every day of his exiſtence, by more than one ſuch deed as this.—Know, ye rich and powerful,

ful, ye who might ſave hundreds of your fellow-creatures, from ſtarving, by the ſweepings of your tables—Know, that, among the various feelings of almoſt every wretch who quits Newgate for Tyburn, a concern neither laſt nor leaſt is that which he feels upon leaving the gaol of which this man is the keeper.

But I can now no longer fly from myſelf. In a few ſhort hours the hand which is now writing to you, the hand which——

I will not diſtreſs either you or myſelf. My life I owe to the laws of my country, and I will pay the debt. How I felt for poor Dodd! Well—you ſhall hear that I died like a man and a chriſtian. I cannot have a better truſt than in the mercy of an all-juſt God. And, in your letters, when you ſhall theſe unhappy deeds relate, tell of me as I am. I forget the paſſage, 'tis in Othello.

You muſt ſuffer me to mention the tenderneſs and greatneſs of mind of my dear B. The laſt moments of my life cannot be better ſpent than in recording this complicated act of friendſhip and humanity. When we parted, a taſk too much for us both, he aſked me if there was any thing for which I wiſhed to live. Upon his preſſing me, I acknowledged I was uneaſy, very uneaſy, leſt

L 2 Lord

Lord S. might withdraw an allowance of 50 pounds a year, which I knew he made to her father. "Then," ſaid B. ſqueezing my hand, burſting into tears, and hurrying out of the room, "I will "allow it him." The affectionate manner in which he ſpoke of my S. would have charmed you. God for ever bleſs and proſper him! and my S. and you! and

(The note which follows was written with a pencil. All that was legible is here preſerved, though the ſenſe is incomplete.)

LETTER LXIV.

To the Same.

My dear Charles,

Farewell for ever in this world! I die a ſincere chriſtian and penitent, and every thing I hope that you can wiſh me. Would it prevent my example's having any bad effect if the world ſhould know how I abhor my former ideas of ſuicide, my crime,

. . . .

. . . . . . will be the beſt judge. Of her

her fame I charge you to be careful. My poor S. will . . . .

Your dying H.

LETTER LXV.

From CHARLES —— Esq.

To General ——.

20 August, 1779.

My dear friend,

The ——— coach, which passes through ——— to-morrow, will leave a large packet for you at the George. When your servant goes to the post, he may enquire for it. The contents are copies of such letters as explain the incredible tale of that poor friend of mine, whom you were kind enough to patronize while he remained in your profession, and to assist in promoting after he quitted it. Your's of the latter end of laſt month on the ſubject of his death, convinces me you will not be angry with me for giving you a ſight of theſe letters. There were *many* more among the papers which he ſealed up for me on the morning of his death; but as they are more private, and leſs neceſſary to the ſtory, I have deſtroyed them.

Your memory will, I know, recollect Rochefoucault's reflection—*Si on juge de l'amour par la plû-part de ſes effets, il reſemble plus á la haine qu' á l'amitiè.*

One very important fact ſtruck me on conſidering this melancholy buſineſs. In our recollection three perſons, either extemporaneouſly or deliberately, have determined to ſhoot, firſt the objects of their fury, and then themſelves—Stirn, who killed Mathews in 1761; Ceppi, whom H. mentions; and poor H. himſelf. They all three ſucceeded in the firſt inſtance, and all three failed in the ſecond.

If what I am told be true, what a ſcene muſt have been exhibited at the Shakeſ-

peare,

oon after the cataſtrophe! H. was
l with a ſight of her body. While
contemplating the effect of his
(for madneſs it ſurely muſt have
'o or three people ruſhed in, who,
too late for the entertainment,
the murder, and came to learn
of the victim. One of theſe im-
y recollected H. —— immediately
ed Miſs ——, was, in fact, Lord
. What a groupe for painting!
it not unneceſſary, when his pic-
lrawn at ſuch full length in theſe
would give you a ſketch of the
man, whom, in ſo many years,
o many different ſcenes, I never
ſion but to love till the moment he
l himſelf. To make reflections on
r, would be to write a volume.
nphlet called "Caſe and Memoirs"
rable buſineſs; and may do that
chief of which H. was aware.

*

true," we are told by the author, "that
own life he had a property; and by the
"laws

" laws of nature, he might have difpofed of it, if
" he pleafed—but, *it may be faid*, he had none in
" Mifs ——'s, and, *as fuch*, that he had no right
" to take it from her. Reafon *may* fupport this
" argument; but is nothing favourable to be faid
" for a man who prefers death to life, becaufe
" that life is made wretched by a capricious and an
" ungrateful woman? Page xi.

How very differently does the poor man himfelf talk in one of his Newgate papers to me, which I have to fent you!

" The torture of my fituation is this, that not a
" word can be faid in my favour, unlefs you will
" fay I am mad. But God knows I poffefs all my
" fenfes and feelings much too exquifitely. Yet
" this is not the part of my crime for which I am
" always moft forry. Often, very often, I confi-
" fider my crime with refpect to the influence it
" may have upon the world. An example repre-
" fented in life by vice, has more effect than a pre-
" cept preached by virtue. No one will imitate
" me in murdering the object of his love, but I
" may be confidered by defpair, or by folly, as
" another precedent in favour of the propriety of
" fuicide. Perhaps, if thefe inftances of defpe-
" rate cowardice did not go out to this country,
" through the channels of our papers, by which

" means

"means they are ſtored up as authorities againſt a "diſappointment or a gloomy day, ſuicide would, "with leſs propriety, be termed an *Angliciſm.* Oh "Charles, could the imperceptible, but indiſputa-"ble, magnetiſm of this part of my ſtory be de-"ſtroyed, could my countrymen know how I abhor "this part of my crime, how thoroughly I was "ever convinced (except during my phrenzy) and "how perfectly I am now perſuaded, that *our own* "*lives are no more at our diſpoſals, than the lives of* "*our fellow creatures,* I ſhould expire in ſomething "leſs of mental torture!"

Worthy ſoul! while we abhor, we pity and reſpect: and ſo will poſterity. That juſtice which condemned thee to death cannot refuſe a ſigh, a tear to thy virtues. Reſt, reſt, perturbed ſpirit! Thy Charles, when time ſhall have a little healed the wound made in his friendſhip, will find ſome way to tell the world thy dying wiſh.

My dear General,

Ever your's

Charles ——.

How

How poor, how rich, how abject, how august,
How complicate, how wonderful, is man!
How passing wonder he who made him such!
Who centered in our make such strange extremes!
From different natures marvelously mixt
Connexion exquisite of distant worlds!
Distinguisht link in beings endless chain!
Midway from nothing to the Deity!
A beam ethereal, sullied and absorpt!
Though sullied and dishonoured, still divine!
Dim miniature of greatness absolute!
An heir of glory! a frail child of dust!
Helpless immortal! Insect infinite!
A worm! a God!—I tremble at myself,
And in myself am lost!

NIGHT THOUGHTS.

FINIS.

LATELY PUBLISHED,

And ſold by the PRINCIPAL BOOKSELLERS in Town and Country.

++++++++++++++++++++++++++

I.

THE SORROWS OF WERTER,

A SENTIMENTAL NOVEL.

IN A SERIES OF LETTERS.

Tranſlated from the German of Mr. GOETHE, and Miſs SEWARD.

Tædet cœli convexa tueri.

☞ After having had the honour of a queen (of France) among the number of his tranſlators, it would be preſumption to offer to the public any encomium on the author of 'The SORROWS of WERTER.' The Publiſher will only obſerve, that it has already been tranſlated into the principal languages of Europe, and received the approbation of every reader of taſte and ſentiment.

Price, 2s. 8d. h. bound.

++++++++++++++++++++++++++++++++++

II.

KISSES OF SECUNDUS,

With a Head of the Author, finely engraved.

Price, 3s. 3d. bound.

++++++++++++++++++++++++++++++++++

III.

OWEN OF CARRON, A POEM.

BY DOCTOR LANGHORNE.

Price, 1s. 1d.

SD - #0017 - 300621 - C0 - 229/152/13 - PB - 9781334936319